Restaurant Confidential

The Down and Dirty Exploits of a Restaurant Manager

By: Daniel Golio

Disclaimer

Restaurant Confidential is a memoir based on actual events. It reflects the author's present recollections of experiences over time. Some names and features been changed to respect their privacy. Any similarity to any person living or dead is merely coincidental.

Some events have been compressed and embellished, and some dialogue has been recreated.

Dedication

This is the fourth book that I have written since I retired from the restaurant industry. In that time, I have dedicated my books to my wife, my mom, and my dad but when I think who made the biggest impact in my life to write my story of working in the restaurant industry it would have to be "MISS DIVA" because she would give me a look with her eyes and her loving smile told me to take pen to paper and write my story about the "Dog Eat Dog World" of the hospitality industry

So, I dedicate this fourth book to MISS DIVA my Chihuahua.

MISS DIVA

Table of Contents

What it's Really Like To Work in The Restaurant Industry?

When I started out in the restaurant business I was a dishwasher in the Back Of the House (B.O.H.) and eventually moved up to 'Sous Chef and then transitioned to the Front Of the House (F.O.H.).

In the B.O.H. you are one of the invisibles or ghosts that no one sees or hears from, and it is not uncommon to work 16-hour shifts, 6 days a week in a hot, 110-degree kitchen with the Chef or Sous Chef screaming out orders.

Working In Restaurants Is Not Glamourous

Working in the back of the house is not the glamourous fun-loving job you see in movies. Not by a long shot, it is long hard work, standing on your feet all day and having the Chefs barking food orders at you or waiters complaining that their food orders are coming out too slow.

Dealing with customers who order a steak medium rare who have no idea what medium rare means, so they send that steak back because they really wanted it medium well.

Or the know-it-all customer who runs the waiter ragged and then leaves no tip for the waiter.

It's a business that you learn while you work, for example, you learn the importance of good fitting shoes and learn how to flash a fake smile at a moment's notice. Or as a line cook you learn to appreciate mini vacations in the walk-in refrigerator and the ability to knock out 50-60 entrees in one hour makes you a superhero.

Working at a restaurant isn't a glamorous job like it is in movies or on TV. Marketing and reality television have wrongly portrayed Chefs as figures of greatness and working in restaurants like a fun social event.

Only a Few Television Chefs Can Cut It

Most of the Chefs you see on some of these cooking shows would not last one day in a real working kitchen. To be successful in a working kitchen you need not only knowledge and talent but timing and speed. I mean almost anyone can work from a recipe and cook an excellent meal but to do it under pressure and bang out 50, 60, or 70 covers an hour and still achieve the same quality in the food is hard and most of these so-called reality chefs would fold under pressure.

For example, one so called Chef was a stockbroker on Wall Street who left his lucrative career on Wall Street during a time when the NASDAQ fell almost 14 percent that year to work in the restaurant business. So, he spent the next few years working as a dishwasher and prep cook working his way up the line. To my knowledge and his bio, he has never worked as a Chef. The restaurant business is hard work, and he soon stopped working in restaurants to suddenly turn up as a Chef on his own cooking show.

He has a fantastic personality and I love his show, but the reality is I don't believe he could bang out 50 covers in an hour if his life depended on it. Not a real Chef!

Of course, television has brought to light Chefs that can or have handled the pressure of a working kitchen like Wolfgang Puck, Michael Lomonaco, Alain Ducasse, Anthony Bourdain, David Bouley, Jessica Largey, and Nadia Santini from Italy to name a few. These are real Chefs and not the reality television personalities that marketing and advertising executives promote as so-called Chefs.

Most of the movies and television shows portray this glamour of attractive women, well to do businessmen and entrepreneurs ready to invest in an unknown Chef.

That's the movies and television for you. Sixty percent of all restaurants fail in the first year and by year four the failure rate is up to eighty percent.

Anyone Can Open a Restaurant

People think to themselves, hey I can cook I can open a restaurant. The restaurant business is just that, a business and you need business experience and real back of the house cooking experience to maybe succeed, if not you will most likely be part of that sixty percent failure rate.

Years ago, I had a few friends who opened a restaurant club combo on the westside of Manhattan in New York City. It was a great place, and a big hit. The club was standing room only, the bar packed and downstairs the 100 seat white tablecloth restaurant was so busy it was reservations only and their restaurant was a very popular place.

Unfortunately, they bought into the television glamour of the restaurant business and used the restaurant as a social event entertaining friends or drinking at the bar. They would be downstairs dining in the restaurant and not paying attention to the business end of the restaurant business. The result is that their restaurant closed within six months after opening.

Being in the hospitality business for such a long period of time you get to learn what to look for. For example, the attractive girls who would take the twenty-dollar admission fee at the door to get into the club would pocket most of that money. Why? No control systems in place.

Food and Beverage Control

A simple control like giving each customer a ticket for a free drink would do the trick because each ticket symbolizes a customer who paid the twenty-dollar entrance fee. Simply multiply the entrance fee times the number of drink tickets and that's how much money the restaurant should have brought in at the door. – Simple!

Observing the bar, I could see that the bartender would not ring up a lot of the bottled beer and or glasses of wine the restaurant sold, and the bartender was only ringing up the hard stuff, vodka, rum, and bourbon.

Had the owners counted the empty beer bottles nightly and compared the empty bottles to the register menu item report which shows how many beers were sold, they would have caught this and following the same procedure for wine sales they could have nipped this problem in the butt. Simple!

And finally, the owners should have invested in an automated system where the items ordered flash on a screen in the kitchen as opposed to using the old hard copy check and dupe system.

By using the old system whereby, a waiter writes the customer's order on a numbered piece of paper called a dupe and brings it in the kitchen for service creates the real possibility for a dishonest waiter to steal.

All checks and dupes are numbered, and each waiter is supposed to sign for a specific number of checks, say you are a waiter, and you sign for checks 1 to 5.

At the end of his shift the waiter should have returned either by sale or unused the 5 checked he signed for.

At the end of the evening the Chef is supposed to match the dupes with the hard copy checks if they don't match you have a thief! – Simple!

However, most Chefs are burnt out at the end of their shift, and they just discard the dupes and never match them with the hard copy checks and the dishonest waiter will take advantage of this, and the door is open to steal.

Basically, if a customer is paying cash for their meal the waiter will drop their check, take the cash, and pocket the money. The waiter then holds that check until another customer has almost the same meal and is paying by credit card. The waiter then rings up the sale with the credit card.

So, the waiter signed for five checks and five checks were returned. Since the dupes and checks are never matched together no one really knows how many times the waiter used the same check and pocketed the money. Simple!

Had these simple control measures been put in place the restaurant might have survived and not become one of the statistical failures of the restaurant business.

High Stress And Substance Abuse

The restaurant business is a high stress industry, and as a result, many employees become alcoholics or drug addicts because of the stress.

COVID 19 made the job harder because of the lack of qualified help, the employees that did stay or got a job in the restaurant business had to work even harder to cover for the lack of qualified help.

In my time I have seen a lot of drug use and heavy drinking. It is estimated that approximately 27 percent of the Chefs working in restaurants today are using alcohol to get thru their workday and another 40 percent are taking some other type of stimulus with the drug of choice being cocaine.

In fact, celebrity Chef Gordon Ramsay says that *Cocaine* is the dirty little secret of the restaurant industry. The widespread substance abuse in the restaurant business is due in part to the long hours, stress, and hard-working conditions the industry puts on its workers.

However, Chefs, managers and the employees who work in this industry do so because they love the work. Chefs do this job because they have a passion for cooking and for them cooking is an expression of art with the plate being the palate.

It's a Different Type of Business

The restaurant industry is also an industry where employees must work together all for a common cause. Getting along is crucial to putting out a good product and satisfying the customer.

Being together 6 days and 70 hours, a week creates not only friendships, but love interests as well.

After my college years nearly all the girlfriends I had were work related in one way or another.

The restaurant industry is different than any other industry in the world. For example, let's say that you go to Macy's department store and pick out a shirt and rather than going to the cashier to pay for it, you decide to wear the shirt in the store to get a feel for the shirt and to see if you like it before buying it.

Most likely Macy's department store would have called security the moment you put the shirt on and started walking around the store. You would have been detained and possibility arrested for attempted shoplifting.

In a restaurant, however, you order your food, it is made and delivered to your table and you eat the food. It is only after you have consumed the product (food) that you are asked to pay for it.

It's different, and many customers know that and try to scam you

I remember this one time a couple ordered an expensive meal with wine in a restaurant I was managing. Then the man suddenly falls to the floor, his mouth foaming, like he was having a heart attack or was deathly allergic to something he ate.

I quickly brought them to the office so as not to make a scene and assured them that the restaurant would comp the meal. They told me that was not enough, and the restaurant should do more for the undue hardship the restaurant caused them.

The only problem was, I had been watching this couple and saw the guy take an Alka Seltzer tablet out of his shirt pocket and put it in his mouth, which immediately caused his foaming at the mouth.

It was an old attempt at not paying the bill, so I played along with this couple and told them that I called the police and an ambulance, which was company policy.

I had not made the calls because I knew about the scam, and just like that they were ready to leave telling me that the free meal was more than adequate.

At which point I put my hand in the guy's shirt pocket and pulled out two Alka seltzer tablets and told him that I would call the police and have them arrested if they don't pay.

So, he tells me that he left his wallet at home and if I let them go he will get his wallet and come back to the restaurant and pay the bill.

I say okay, but you will have to leave your wife as collateral. If you don't return with payment she goes to jail. He says deal.

His wife says he won't be back, and she was right, he gave her up and did not return.

I felt bad for her that her own husband, or so she says he was, would not return for his wife so I let her go.

But I did not let the scammers get off that easy. I had this woman give me her high heels and made her walk home barefoot. I mean somebody must pay.

Why People Go To Restaurants

Customers frequent restaurants for many reasons. Here are some reasons why people go to restaurants: The restaurant is a place to socialize, unwind and have fun. It is a break from the normal routine, or it can be a place to conduct business and it is also a place to try new foods or to have foods you cannot cook at home.

Also, when people like to celebrate say a birthday, anniversary or any special event, the restaurant is usually the place to go.

Basically, a restaurant should be a place of fun, free from stress however some restaurants are quite the opposite.

In a recent survey by a well-known restaurant magazine, customers rated what that disliked most about restaurants.

Customers disliked restaurants that packed them together like sardines with cramped tables and hardly enough room to enjoy their meal.

Restaurants that charge a lot for their food and claim it's made fresh but serve frozen and or precooked steam table food is a real turn off.

At the top of the list is poor customer service, be it poor knowledge of the restaurant menu or lack of attention to the customers' needs or the restaurant policy of only one check per table.

Believe it or not the survey found that cleanliness and food safety was ranked somewhere in the middle of the survey.

Take New York City for example, it has its health department letter system, with A being best and so on, but did you know that there are 25,000 restaurants in the City of New York and only one hundred restaurant inspectors?

Thats right, only one hundred inspectors per 25,000 restaurants. Do the math, that works out to 250 restaurants per health inspector. Still feeling your favorite restaurant is safe to eat in?

The fact is that rodents, bugs, poor holding temperatures and poor hygiene can make customers physically sick. Restaurants with these problems are not closed but are given time to correct these above issues while the restaurant is open for business.

The Real World

So, what is it like to work in the restaurant industry. It is sore feet, getting yelled at by customers, and if you work in the back of the house you always smell like garlic and onions.

It is hard work for little pay. If you calculate that the average Chef makes around $75,000 per year and divide that by 52 weeks and his or her 60-hour work week that averages out to an hourly wage of around $24.00. Let's face it the average wage of a plumber is $36.00 per hour.

Of course, becoming the General Manager or the Director of Food and Beverage pays a great deal more money, it is still long hard work.

I have been around food all my life and learned to cook at an early age. When I was in my early teens my dad worked two jobs and my mom had to work to make ends meet. I learned to cook very early in life so going into the restaurant business was only natural.

I have always liked the excitement and hustle and bustle of the restaurant business; From my time as a Sous Chef to being the Director of Food and Beverage, to owning my catering company, and finally teaching others about the restaurant industry, restaurants have always been in my blood.

Astor Italian Restaurant

Four days a week I would go to the Astor Italian Restaurant located at 2300 Eastchester Road, Bronx, NY 10469 which was just minutes from my home and work from 4:00 pm until 10: pm. I worked Saturday to Sunday and Tuesday to Wednesday.

I started out as the dishwasher. Then I graduated to the dishwasher and clam shucker. When I came to work, I would wash all the pots and dishes, then start my prep for the evening which was cleaning shrimp, and shucking oysters and clams.

It was hard work, but I enjoyed working in the kitchen. We had four employees in the kitchen: The Chef, Sous Chef, a line cook and me. I was sixteen years old at the time and I had no idea what I was going to do with my life. By the time I was eighteen I was a line cook banging out entrees left and right.

It was the late 1960's and the Chef, who was in his mid-twenties, was sort of like a Hippie. He was a long-hired skinny guy that was a vegetarian. I had no idea what a vegetarian was at the time and found it strange that he was in a restaurant that served mainly meat, you know, Veal, Pork, and Chicken dishes.

He wore sandals and beads and advocated nonviolence and love. He smoked Weed and did recreational drugs when he was not working.

In the kitchen he would play the music of Bob Dylan, or the Rolling Stones as we worked, while the dining room had the sounds of Frank Sinatra, Dean Martin, or Jerry Vale.

I learned a lot from him like the proper way to cut an Onion or how not to overcook Broccoli.

At the Astor Italian restaurant, I learned one of the most important rules of the restaurant business which was that without dishes you cannot serve the guests.

So, next to the Chef, the second most important person in the kitchen is the dishwasher. I mean if you have no dishes to plate the food on, service stops – Period end of story.

During the summer months the restaurant closed at 11:00 pm but kept the bar food open until 1:00 am.

I worked the late-night shift during the summer months making sandwiches for the bar; you know chicken parmesan sandwich or a meatball hero and of course an Italian sub sandwich (Salami, Capicola and Provolone). Our bread came from the Terranova Bakery on Arthur Avenue in the Bronx – The real deal!

One night in July I am making an Italian sub sandwich and as I cut the Genoa salami, I comment to myself how fresh the salami is. We purchased all our cold cuts from the Boars Head company, which made the best cold cuts back then and the salami was bright red.

Then I looked at the slicer and it was full of blood, my blood, The electric slicer was so sharp that I did not even feel it when it cut half of my right thumb off.

Frantic, I start to search for the top half of my right thumb which I find on the floor near the walk-in refrigerator. Remembering a show on saw on PBS, I get a Styrofoam cup, fill it with ice and put the top half of my right thumb in the ice. Wrapping my hand with a kitchen towel I told the bar manager what happened, and I walked to Jacobi hospital which was only a few blocks away.

Once inside I go to the emergency room and show them my thumb. They handed me papers to fill out to see if I had insurance. I did not, but they said your company will cover it because the injury is work related.

With my hand wrapped in a kitchen towel and blood dripping onto to the hospital floor I wait for the doctor.

When I see the doctor, he says "How did you know to put your thumb on ice?"

I tell him about the show I saw on PBS, and he says, "Thank God for PBS – Right!"

"Yea" I say as he tapes my thumb together and tells me not to get it wet.

It's my senior year of high school, I'm eighteen and I'm now the Sous Chef at the restaurant. I have been cooking at the Astor Italian Restaurant for almost two years.

After high school I continued to work as the Sous Chef of the Astor Italian Restaurant for another three years.

St. Raymond's High School For Boys

I went to St. Raymonds High School, a parochial school which was separated by two buildings: St. Raymond's High School for Boys and St. Raymond's High School for Girls. The Boys high school was run by the De La Salle Christian Brothers.

When I went to St. Raymonds, Brother Andrew was the principal of the boy's high school.

Mostly all the De La Salle Christian Brothers were Irish: Brother Andrew, Brother Brendan, Brother Byrne, Brother Rearden all Irish.

While I was an A+ student I managed to make the list of the top 10 ten worst kids in the school.

Every year Brother Andrew would announce the names of the worst kids in the school, and I made the list every year not because I had poor grades, I made the list because I stood up for the weaker kids and was always getting into some sort of fight.

Anyway, in my last year of high school I was taking a course in Business mathematics. I was doing well in class with a B+ average but the teacher who was also Irish did not like me and told me something to the effect

" I don't care how good your grades are, I not going to pass you. All you Italians are alike" he says

I went home and told my dad what happened. The next week I am in class and my business math teacher walks up to me and in front of the whole class he grabs me by my shirt collar and says is a low voice in my ear:

"You think I'm intimidated by you Italian thugs; all you Italians are disgusting"

I have no idea what he is talking about but apparently my dad made a phone call to some people he knows, and they went to talk to my Mathematics teacher about me passing his class - Real Godfather stuff.

Anyway, he is shaking me by my collar and screaming at me in front of the whole class. I clinch my fists to hit him in self-defense, but I don't; instead, I use my brains

I say to him" Go ahead, hit me I know you want to" "Do it or are you a coward!"

His Irish face gets beet red, and I can see that he is really thinking about hitting me. The whole class is watching him as he raises his hand to strike me, but then he stops and says to me

"Go to the Vice principal's office NOW"

I leave the classroom, but I do not go straight to the Vice principal's office but to a pay phone in the lobby of the school and call the police and tell them what happened and that I have been assaulted by my teacher.

Then I go to the Vice Principal's office to wait, the door is locked and like most schools you sit outside the Vice Principals office until he or she comes, and you tell him why you are sitting there.

A few minutes later I told the Vice Principal that I was attacked by the mathematics teacher and I'm here to make a complaint. Within minutes the police arrive, and the action really starts.

The police pulled the mathematics teacher out of class and all of us were in Brother Andrew's office to discuss the matter.

So, I told my side of what happened and that all 25 students in the class saw it. My teacher says very little except to say that he might have gotten a little carried away, but I did not hurt Mr. Golio

I was a senior and I was eighteen years old, so the police said to me "What do you want to do? Are you going to file a complaint against him or what?

Just then Brother Andrew says to the police

"Let me talk to the boy alone if that's okay"

"Okay with you son" the police say

"Yea okay" I say

Alone in Brother Andrew's office he says to me"

"Listen I don't like Italians and I don't like you!"

"Think of the school, we don't need any bad publicity so drop this and you will graduate with honors."

"What about my Business class" I say.

Well, you a have a B+ average so let's say that will be your final grade." Okay?" Brother Andrew says.

"Okay, but I want an apology" I say

We leave the principal's office, I shake hands with my math teacher, he apologies, the police leave, and everyone is happy. I graduated with honors.

The high school was okay but gave me little direction as to what I wanted to do with my life. So, as I mentioned, I worked as the Sous Chef of the Astor Restaurant for another three years.

I really enjoyed cooking, and I enjoyed feeding people and seeing the smile on their face when they liked what I cooked. I always thought of the dinner plate as a canvass by which to display my culinary art and always preferred a white dinner plate to do so.

So, for me, being the Sous Chef in an Italian restaurant was work I really enjoyed. It was satisfying work and the money was good, so I was happy.

Eventually my parents told me that I needed a college education. So, I decided to go to New York

Technical College at 300 Jay St in Brooklyn and get a degree in Culinary Arts and Restaurant management.

New York Technical College

The days were long and since I was still living in the Bronx with my parents, I had to travel on the #5 train to Jay Street and Borough Hall to get to school. The ride took over 1 hour, so it was a very long and tiring day.

The first week my culinary instructor, Professor Veal told the class to make a sheath for our knives to make carrying the knives easier.

One day I was on the #5 train at 5:00 am traveling to my morning Culinary Arts class and this girl in a short skirt gets on the train and sits opposite me.

On the train at this hour was me, the girl, and an old lady around sixty years of age.

At the next stop, a teenager around sixteen or seventeen gets on the train. He starts tormenting the girl by groping her and pulling on her dress.

She moves her seat, but he follows her and continues to feel her up. You could see tears in her eyes and that look that says please help me.

The old lady says to me to do something. I do nothing and he continues to harass the girl. Finally, he starts to pull her panties down and she starts to scream.

I stand up and say to him" Leave her alone and why don't you just cut this"

He looks at me and pulls out a pocketknife with about a four-inch blade and says to me

"Man, sit down and be quiet or you will get hurt"

I am now in the heat of it, so I pull out my 10-inch chef's knife and say "Listen man - THIS IS A KNIFE! and move towards him.

He sees the knife and starts running into the next car. Like a fool I follow him and just then the train stops at the149th street station, and he runs out of the train. A transit policeman is standing in the doorway of the train with his gun drawn. I dropped the knife and told him what happened. We go to the next car so the old lady and the girl can back up my story, but they have left.

At the police station I called the school, and my professor vouched for me, and the transit police let me go – Don't help people you don't know - Lesson learned.

In college I had a great time, learned a lot from the culinary professors like Professor Veal or Professor Busetti and learned about managing a dining room from Professor McHugh (Irish).

It would be Professor Veal and Professor McHugh that would change my direction in life and put me on the right road to my career goals.

At the college we took courses not only in culinary arts and baking but in food and beverage management and hospitality management as well. I learned a great deal here at New York Technical College and made some great long-lasting friends both private and professional.

Dan Golio with friends Stephany Kameko and Kin-Chung-Yiu

The college had graduated some celebrity chefs and entrepreneurs as well. For Example, Japanese entrepreneur Hiroaki "Rocky" Aoki was an alumnus who graduated from the college in 1963 with a degree in Culinary Arts and Restaurant Management.

At one of the alumni reunions, I had the opportunity to meet and talk with him. Rocky, started his now world famous Benihana restaurants corporation with only $10,000 which was money he made while driving an ice cream truck in all places "Harlem."

You know I was born and raised in Harlem – go figure!

Rocky Aoki

That first Benihana restaurant located on West 56th Street would go on to spark a business worth millions of dollars.

He founded the "Rocky Aoki Award" for the senior who showed the greatest amount of growth at the college.

Rocky Aoki was a true entrepreneur who not only was a successful restaurant entrepreneur but a man who created "Genesis", a men's magazine that lasted well after his death in 2008.

Alumni Michael Lomonaco best known for his television cooking shows, and cookbooks graduated from New York Technical College a few years after me.

Years later he would open his restaurant "Windows On The World" in the World Trade Center which would be destroyed in the terrorist attacks on that building on September 11, 2001.

At the time of the attacks, I was a professor teaching at the Art Institute of New York City just five blocks away and witnessed the devastation firsthand.

One of the original Food Network and Travel Channel Chef personalities with his shows Michael's Place and Epicurious, Michael Lomonaco opened his world-famous Porter House Bar and Grill in 2006, which is located at 10 Columbus Circle, 4th floor New York, NY 10019. The restaurant was voted the "Best Steak House in New York" by the "New Yorker Magazine."

An excerpt from the New Yorker Magazine describes Michale Lomonaco's Porter House Bar and Grill as follows: *"A restaurant with first-class service, opulent side dishes, grand wines, and traditional and trendy cuts of beef — Michael Lomonaco's Columbus Circle restaurant remains the gold standard for the postmillennial, chef-driven, fat-cat New York steakhouse. "- Adam Platt"*

Chef Michael LoMonaco

Lomonaco survived the attack of September 11th because he was in the lobby of the building at the time of the attacks, but his entire staff, that day of which many were students from my classes at the Art Institutes did not, and all were killed in the terrorist attacks.

Anyway, while I was still in college, I held my Sous Chef position for the three weeks of college but eventually my college courses interfered with the hours at the restaurant, so I had to quit and seek other employment.

When I graduated from New York Technical College I took a full-time management position with Nedick's Corporation.

Nedick's Food Stores

The Nedick's chain was founded by Robert T. Neely, a real estate investor, and Orville A. Dickinson. The original Nedick's stand opened in a hotel storefront at the Bartholdi Hotel in 1913. In the 1970's the company was purchased by the Ogden Corporation of Manhattan.

When I decided to go to college to make the hospitably industry my career, I had to quit my job as a Sous Chef in the Italian restaurant I was working at because the night hours conflicted with my college class schedule.

I landed a job as the breakfast cook with Nedick's foodservice who at the time was known for its signature orange drink and Sabrett® hot dogs, with a unique mustard relish in a toasted bun.

Nedick's operated full-service coffee shops and multi-unit operations in the Port Authority Bus Terminal in New York City as well as Penn and Grand Central stations.

Interestingly a lot of my food service positions put me in either the Port Authority of New York, or Penn and Grand Central Station. I mean I could have been a tour guide.

Anyway, every morning at 5:00 am I was working the flat grill in Penn station turning out omelets, eggs any style, pancakes, bacon, and toasted bagels. Cooking here was a one-man operation – Me

Before I left my shift, I was responsible for making tuna and chicken salads for the lunch rush. The Nedick's way was to take stale unseeded rye bread and mix it into the salads thus doubling the volume of the salads. So, if you ever wonder how deli restaurants can give you a large portion of tuna or chicken salad for the money. Hey – there you go!

After graduation I was asked by the Director of Personnel of Nedick's Corporation to join their management team. I agreed and was placed in the Port Authority Bus Terminal on 42nd and 8th avenue. Since I was already an experienced breakfast cook for the company for 2 years, training was very basic, just showing me how to close the cash registers, take inventory and complete the daily sales reports.

With that I got my first unit, a small place that served mainly hot dogs, orange drink, donuts, coffee, and soda. I had three employees.

Nedick's - Port Authority

At the time the Port authority was a dirty, dangerous place. I mean it was a breeding ground of pimps, prostitutes, pickpockets, and drug addicts.

I remember one morning I am working the counter and these two women, obviously prostitutes say to me that they will give me a BJ for a couple of hot dogs.

I look at my employee standing next to me, and he gives me the nod to take them into the walk-in refrigerator. I shake my head and say" That's not my thing."

I told them thanks but no thanks and gave the two prostitutes a hot dog each and told them not to come back.

The Port Authority on 42nd street and 8th avenue was a nasty place to work. One day an old woman is walking towards the #2 train and a guy grabs her handbag and darts for the stairs, just then, a homeless man who was sleeping in the corner not too far from my unit jumps up.

"Police", he yells, exposes his shield, and shoots his 45-caliber pistol twice at the fleeing purse snatcher.

Just then, two other undercover police officers jump up and grab the guy. I mean it was like this almost all the time. Pimps would hunt for naive girls just arriving from busses coming from the Midwest, drugs were sold in plain view and crime was rampant in bellows of the Port Authority Bus Terminal.

Attrition was high in the management department, and within a few months I was now in charge of all fifteen foodservice units between the Port Authority Bus Terminal, Penn, and Grand Central station. I am not saying that I was such a great manager and upper management noticed my management skills, no it was most likely that I was one of the few remaining managers with the most seniority.

Nedick's Franks

We had a large coffee shop at the entrance of the train station and into the Port Authority Bus Terminal. One day I was standing at the cashier stand talking to the cashier and this guy runs right past me to the back of the restaurant and immediately following him are two other guys, they were plain clothes police with their guns drawn yelling at the guy they were chasing to stop.

The guy stopped and the police handcuffed him and took him out of my restaurant. Apparently he had ripped a gold chain from a woman who had just gotten off the train. Undercover police spotted the incident, and the chase began.

Back then subway trains were covered in graffiti, inside and out. Crime was rampant. Women were warned to remove jewelry while walking the streets for fear that their necklaces would be ripped from their necks.

Pimps, robbery, rape, and drugs with an occasional hot dog thrown in. This period in New York City was not one of its finest moments, it was one of the bleakest, most crime-ridden, and most uncertain periods the city has ever faced.

At the time Ogden Corporation of Manhattan ran all the food and beverage operations at Yonkers and

Belmont raceway where business was booming. At the Port Authority Bus Terminal plans were in the works for a total overall of the terminal. Under Mayor Ed Kotch renovation began to overall the entire station.

The Ogden Corporation of Manhattan made the decision not to renew its license for Nedick's stores in the soon to be newly renovated bus terminal and subsequently closed all Nedick's stores to concentrate on its Raceway food service operations.

Although I was offered a position as a Food and Beverage Manager at Yonkers raceway, I decided to venture out and get a job at JFK International Airport. I figured I have a Restaurant and Culinary Arts degree, four years of multi-unit food and beverage management experience as well as Sous Chef experience so I am the perfect candidate for the job – at least that is what I thought!

JFK International Airport

When I left Nedick's corporation I took a few weeks off and then I applied for a food and manger position at Host International at John F. Kennedy International Airport (JFK) in Queens, New York.

During the summer months travel is at its peak at most airports so many foodservice companies hire management for the summer and if they work out, permanent positions are offered to the managers they feel are best.

I applied for a Food and Beverage manager position but did not get the job. I had thought the interview went well and my experience was a perfect fit for the job, so I was dumfounded that I was not hired.

Thinking back on the interview I said to myself maybe they think I'm too young for the job. During the early years I did look young for my age, so I grew a mustache and applied again. This time I got the job.

I was to work in the East wing of the International Arrivals building and was given two snack bars and two bars to manage, easy considering that I had come from managing 15 food and beverage units at the Bus Terminal at the Port Authority in New York City. The training required was to learn their computer systems and paperwork.

The Food and Beverage manager position involved a lot of walking, standing and very long hours. Basically, making change for the cashiers and bartenders, handling customer complaints and watching the cashiers and bartender so they don't steal and of course closing out the registers and doing the company paperwork.

The restaurant business is a tough business and while many want to be the boss and manage, few have the endurance and the street smarts to succeed. As a result, most of the college students that get hired as management trainees quit and the more experienced managers either get burned out or quit because of the long grueling hours.

At an airport, especially JFK International Airport, planes get delayed and cancelled all the time and passengers who must wait around the airport head straight for the bars or restaurants. That means foodservice operations stay open later and a manager's shift gets longer. It was not unusual for me to put in an 18-hour day; sometimes these 18-hour days went for three or four days in a row.

Within three months I was managing both the East and West wing of the International Arrivals Building and by the end of the year I was the Food and Beverage Director for all food and beverage operations for Host International at JFK International Airport.

While it was hard work it was a fun time for me. I was kind of a late bloomer when it came to women, but JFK International Airport changed all that.

JFK is More Than Work

During this time most of the employees were around the same age give or take a few years. Only the General Manager of Airport Operations was much older. He was tall and thin and a man who enjoyed his Weed. When you entered his office the smell of Weed permeated the air. He was also a Richard Nixon supporter, so just like Nixon, when you entered his office, he recorded all his conversations.

Anyway, many of the management were dating cocktail waitress and cashiers, not me, I started dating stewardesses, I mean, I'm in the International Arrivals Building and the United Terminal so there were stewardesses from all over the world: France, Italy, Sweden, Jamaica, and the United States. My mother raised no fool.

At that time stewardesses could fly anywhere their airline flew and just pay the tax on the airline ticket. And that went for the stewardess family as well. So, I hooked up with a stewardess from United Airlines named Arlene and I would travel like her brother and fly to Miami, Florida, every other weekend for practically nothing.

Of course, dating a stewardess had more than just flying perks. A new English low-cost airline had come into the airline business called Laker Airways. It was a British airline founded by Sir Freddie Laker and became one of the first low-cost, "no frills" airlines in 1977, operating low-fare scheduled services between London Gatwick Airport and John F. Kennedy International Airport. To me it was an airline with a lot of kinks to work out. I believe Laker had only four McDonnell-Douglas DC-10 wide bodied jets and these aircraft were almost always delayed.

During this time, I was dating a black girl named Angie, she was one of the supervisors for Laker Airways. One night she called me to tell me that the NY to London flight would be delayed indefinitely and to expect a lot of angry passengers. Apparently, engine trouble shut down the aircraft.

If you ever took a flight anywhere, you most likely would look at the flight board to see what gate your plane is leaving from and whether it is on time or not.

The Laker policy was to show a plane that was delayed as "On Time" then as time got close to take off time, change the status to "Delayed" and finally to "See agent."

Angie was hot, fun and I really liked her, but she was relocated to the London office, my loss and London's gain.

Many airlines give out vouchers to delayed passengers and the passengers bring these vouchers to airport restaurants to exchange them for food. However, airlines like Laker Airways never tell the passengers that the voucher does not cover the cost of a meal or that once you give that voucher to the cashier you lose it. I mean if you don't know this you might only want to get a coffee or a soda now, thinking I'll come back later for food. However, once you give your voucher in anything else you might want later you need to pay for out of your own pocket because the voucher is a one-time use.

Everybody Has To Pay

Part of the job as I mentioned was customer service and dealing with passengers. I remember one time in the International Arrivals Building I had a customer who did not want to pay for her sandwich. She had ordered a hot Pastrami sandwich and a beer.

This was in our full-service restaurant, and I asked the manager on duty what's the problem. He told me that the customer did not like the sandwich and was not going to pay.

I approach the customer and I Say "Hi, I'm the Food and Beverage Director, what seems to be the problem"

She is an attractive girl in her early twenties wearing a low-cut blouse and very sexy. She says to me" The sandwich was not any good, it was fatty and tasteless, and I should not have to pay for it"

I looked at her plate and saw that the entire sandwich was eaten, even the pickle and potato chips, and her beer glass was empty as well. Then I look back at her and I say to her "If the sandwich did not taste good why did you eat it?"

She looks me dead in the face her eyes lashes batting and with a pouty face says to me:

"Well, I took a bite, and it did not taste good, so I took another bite and then another bite in hopes the sandwich would taste better but when I finished eating the sandwich it did not taste any better than when I started, so I should not have to pay."

I put my face inches from her face and said to her in a soft whisper "Lady, if you don't have an Andrew Jackson in that purse you are going to jail."

Immediately she pulls out a twenty-dollar bill from her purse and puts it down on the table and saunters away, turning around she says to me "Well you can't blame a girl for trying."

Shaking my head, I picked up the check and the twenty-dollar bill hand it to the manager and continued my tour of the restaurants and bars in the East and West wing of the International Arrivals Building.

I mean it was like that, customers would try not to pay all the time. I remember once at the United Terminal there was this guy that never paid. Let's call him Mr. Dine and Dash, which is a person who eats at a restaurant and then runs away without paying.

Anyway, if management approached Mr. Dine and Dash, he would make a scene, so they left him alone. He always got over. That was until he met ME!

At the United Terminal we had a full-service restaurant that was situated like a buffet, you could order an entrée that was made fresh, like fried chicken or something, then take items from the buffet like salads, drinks, desserts, and so forth and in the middle of the restaurant was a cashier that you had to pass by to get to the dining room tables.

So, I watch this guy and he orders fried chicken with fries, and a cheeseburger with fried onion rings and from the buffet he takes a chef salad and an apple pie for dessert.

He walks right past the cashier and sits in the back of the restaurant and begins eating. While he is eating his fried chicken, I approach his table and say to him in a low pleasant voice

"Excuse me I noticed that you forgot to pay for your meal. Maybe you did not see the cashier." Would you mind paying when you finish your meal."

He looks up at me and says" Man, I don't pay, I never pay" - "Go Away" and continues eating his fried chicken."

I walked away and called my friend John, who was head of the Port Authority Police at JFK and told him I got a guy that doesn't want to pay, and I want him arrested.

John says to me "Dan, that's a big deal, first you must sign a complaint then we got to arrest him and then book him and then you got go to court and testify - you really want to do this thing?

I say, "Yea John, I want this guy arrested."

John says" Okay great we are kind of bored down here anyway."

By now the Mr. Dine and Dash is on his dessert, a freshly baked apple pie from our commissary. John on the other hand is in the kitchen with 10 port authority police officers all dressed in their swat gear complete with shot guns.

I approach Mr. Dine and Dash one last time and say, "I hope you enjoyed your meal now it's time to pay"

He looks at me and says, "You are a stupid motherfucker, I told you I don't pay" Get the fuck out of my face man!"

I say to him "So you are not going to pay?"

"Yea man that right, now Fuck off" he says

I raised my hand and snapped my fingers and just like that 10 port authority police rushed to the dining room. They grab Mr. Dine and Dash out of his chair and throw him up against the wall, he is in shock as they handcuff him and tell him to move it.

Handcuffed and with shot guns pointing at him he is slowly lead out of the dining room,

I look at him and say" Who's the stupid motherfucker now!"

I Go Undercover

During the summer Host would usually hire more staff to help with the increase in customers due to the increase in passengers flying. At the time I was dating a girl named Paula who had a friend who wanted to be a cashier.

I was looking for a day cashier and this woman sounded perfect. She had McDonald's experience, and she was in her mid-twenties and her husband was a Sargent at the 107th police department in Queens, New York.

So, I set up an interview for this woman named Mary with the manager. He liked her and he hired her. Things were going great with Mary and the manager had no complaints. Then one day I am doing a walk thru in the United Terminal and Mary approaches me an says to me

"Listen Dan, I know you and Paula are going together so I think can trust you"

"Of course," I say

"Well, I am stealing $200.00 per day, and I need to steal $800.00 per day of which I will give you $200.00 per day what do you say" she says.

Well, I'm no fool so I say to her "This conversation never took place and I'm not going to fire you because you are a friend of Paula, but you need to stop this immediately" and I walk away.

When I get home, I tell Paula about my conversation with Mary and Paula says

"Wow! "My friendship with her is not worth losing your job over so if you want to fire her go ahead."

I started thinking that maybe someone was trying to set me up, so I decided to tell my boss, the General Manager about my conversation with Mary.

The next day I go into his office and the smell of weed permeates the room, coughing from the smoke I tell him the conversation and ask him what do you want to do? He tells me he will think about it.

It's two o clock in the morning when my phone rings at my Kew Gardens apartment. I roll over and answer it and the General Manger is on the line and he says to meet him in the United Terminal parking lot in 30 minutes. I look at Paula and she says" You better go Dan; you know how he is when he has too much weed"

I get dressed, hop into my Plymouth Satellite and head for the airport. When I arrived, there was only a white van parked in the parking lot. I parked next to the van and got out of my car. I then bang on the door of the van; it slides open and marijuana smoke hits my face. "Get in the van" the General Manager says.

He then introduces me to a private detective from the company and both start to tell me that they need to know how Mary is stealing the money.

The private detective asks me "Would you mind wearing a wire?"

Before I could answer "The General Manager says, "No problem, Dan has no problem wearing a wire." Right!"

" I guess not" I respond.

Then they proceed to wire me up and show me how the thing works.

So that Monday I put on a tie clasp which is a miniature microphone that is connected to a mini-tape recorder which is taped to my waist, and I head for work on Monday morning.

I approach Mary and tell her I'm in, and that I could make some extra money too. So, it is now a go. I am now Dan the undercover man!

The airport is a seven-day 24-hour operation, so you need to have three shift scheduling for all the employees as well as management and while I have an assistant manager in the restaurant at the United Terminal, I cover two days a week sort of like a sixth man on Monday and Tuesday. So, that's when Mary steals, on my shift.

For my share of the money, I am to collect it and put in the safe until the end of her shift then we split it, $200.00 for me and $600.00 for her. Easy Peasy!

The way it works is that during her shift, like all cashiers, the cashier will need change you know; quarters, dimes or one-dollar bills. When I give her the needed change, she gives me the $800.00 take for the day which I put in the safe until the end of Mary's shift as we agreed.

By now Host International had their spotters in the restaurant daily. A spotter is a trained individual who observes cashiers, bartenders, and other employees, watching for telltale signs of theft and misconduct. They found nothing, absolutely nothing!

In fact, the spotter's reports showed that Mary was an exceptional cashier. Reports said she was efficient, pleasant, and helpful with no signs of stealing or misconduct of any kind.

So, my General Manager is showing these reports to me and tells me that maybe I got it all wrong.

I say to him "Really! So, what about the $5,000 sitting in your safe!" What about that!"

"Okay, yea I see what you mean." he says

Then he says to me" Let's put an end to this soon if you can't catch her, we will just fire her and be done with it."

So, after four months of this, I tell Mary "Listen I think we should quit this; we are going to get caught." It's too dangerous and besides I don't even know how you are doing this - NO I'm out."

Mary says" Come on, we are not going to get caught for God's sake!"

Then Mary proceeds to tell me "Look see that guy over there he is a spotter and the woman over there she a spotter and even that couple standing over next to the condiment station, they are spotters."

"I look at her and say, "How do you know that?"

"Because spotters are cheap, they only buy a cup of coffee or a soda or at most an order of French fries and a soda – easy."

Then Mary says, "Let me show you how I do it."

I then take my microphone tie clasp and literally put it in her face and say to her – "Tell me!"

"Watch!" she says, as a guy walks up to the register with his tray. He has a Meatloaf dinner consisting of two slices of meatloaf, mashed potatoes and gravy and a bottled beer for a cost of $6.25.

"You saw that I rung up that order right Dan."

"Yea" I say.

"Well, I didn't, I had the cash register drawer almost closed but not completely so that the cash register drawer made contact with the computer's digital display thus displaying the items being rung up, but on this computerized casher register system, the cash register drawer must be completely closed in order for the sale to actually ring up and get recorded in the register. - Got it" Mary says, as she smiles and hands me another wad of cash.

The next day I go to the General manager's office, open the door, and get hit with the strong smell of Weed as it penetrates my nostrils and makes me cough.

I tell the General Manager here is the tape with how she was stealing the money and plop it on his desk.

As he listens to the tape, he is rolling another weed cigarette and says "Great work, Dan! "I'm going to give the tape to personal and have them fire her and then I'm going to tell corporate about the flaws in the Data Computer Register Systems."

On that Friday, Paula gets a call from Mary telling Paula she got fired, but that she did not give me up and it's okay because she made over $20,000 in less than 4 months.

However, it get better for Mary because soon after she applies for unemployment insurance. Apparently, the personnel department at Host International fired Mary for poor cash handling and not stealing so she was able to collect unemployment insurance for the next six months – go figure!

The Blackout of 1977

The blackout of 1977 was caused by a lightning strike that hit a power station in Westchester County and blacked out New York City for more than 25 hours. Time magazine dubbed the blackout as "The Night of Terror" with stores being looted and burned, robberies, rape, and murder. Over 300 million dollars of damage was reported and at JFK International Airport it was no different.

On July 13, 1977, at around 9:15 pm I am in the International Arrivals Building (I.A.B.) doing a walk-through to ensure that the food units and bars that usually close at 9:00 pm were indeed closed. I was nearing the end of my shift and my girlfriend Paula was going to pick me up in my car and we were going to go to her parents' place in Vermont for a four-day mini-vacation.

Suddenly, the lights in the building start to flicker and at 9:30 pm the building is totally dark. The back up lights come on and I head for the main restaurant in the United Terminal of the airport. At the restaurant I look out the window and see that the whole airport is out. The airport has blacked out.

Blackout of 1977

I called my girlfriend, and she told me that not only has the borough of Queens blacked out but all of New York City has blacked out as well.

She says she does not want to stay alone in our apartment in Kew Gardens and that she will come to the airport. I say okay but be careful driving.

Kew Gardens is only 5 miles from the airport and a 10 minute drive by car, so we picked it because of its closeness to her parents and the airport. Her parents lived in Forrest Hills, Queens, which is only 2 miles from Kew Gardens, so it was a perfect location for us.

Within one hour the backup lighting system failed and the airport was totally dark. Being a manager, the first thing you learn is to get the money, so I had all my management staff pull the gates in front of each bar and food operation and collect the money from the patrons.

At all the food, beverage and even gift shops at the airport we had gates that could be pulled down and close the operations so I had management close them so customers could not do a dine and dash (eat and not pay the bill).

With that accomplished I put the money in the safe and sent home my management and all my staff except for two porters to help clean up.

All my food and beverage units closed at 9:00pm so the only operation open was the main restaurant and the bar in the United Terminal, which I now closed.

I opened the gift shop and took out all the I Love NY flashlights and gave them to my employees and kept two for myself and went to check operations. I found two women in their early twenties smoking cigarettes sitting on bar stools from my United Airlines bar.

I said, 'Excuse me but you can't sit on these, they belong to the United Terminals bar."

"Fuck off" was the reply as they continued to smoke and laugh.

"Look, it has United Terminal stamped on the back" I said

"So, who cares, we are not giving them back so fuck off" they said in unison

I returned with my two porters and pulled the chairs from under them, causing them to plop on their asses. Then I gave each of them a six pack of bottle beer and told them to find some place safe.

By that time my girlfriend had arrived so now there were four of us. My girlfriend worked as a cashier during the day, so she was well versed in the operations of the airport.

The plan was to clean up the restaurant and ride out the blackout until morning, and then take four days off and go to Vermont for a mini- vacation.

With the entire city and the airport blacked out, all flights were cancelled and literally thousands of people were roaming the airport in search of shelter and comfort.

Unfortunately for us, the Port Authority of New York and New Jersey drove two large trucks into the main entrance of the United Terminial and turned on their lights, flooding the building with light.

Doing so awakened people who were sleeping or huddled together, and these people decided that food and drink was what they needed, so hundreds of people stormed the gates of my restaurant and bar.

It was like a horde of locusts swarming through a corn field or a scene from "The Walking Dead" - Frightening. This mob was pulling and banging on the gates shouting they wanted food and drink.

While this was going on I found a family of four huddled in the corner of my restaurant dining room, they pleaded with me to allow them to stay in the restaurant and not throw them to the screaming horde outside the gates.

Being a manager and coming from Pleasant Avenue's "Little Italy", I knew how to make a buck, so I said, "Okay you guys can stay but you have to work - understand."

"Yes," they said. "What do you want us to do" they replied

I showed the father how to use the grill and make hamburgers, the mother how to make ham and cheese sandwiches and the two sons who looked to be about fifteen or sixteen how to make coffee and fry chicken and French fries. Paula, being a cashier, handled the money.

The two porters got the beer and cigarettes from the bar, and we put everything in large holding cabinets with wheels and went outside the restaurant to face the horde of hungry people.

They say that supply and demand dictates the price of almost anything. With that being said, we sold a hamburger and fries or fried chicken and fries for $5.00, keep in mind the price in 1977 was an average of $1.50 and we sold beer for $2 per bottle where the average price was $1.00. Coffee and a sandwich was also $2.00. However, if you just wanted coffee, it was free of charge. Cigarettes were $1.00 dollar each. Within two hours we were sold out. Well, that is what supply and demand is all about!

Since the electricity was out all purchases were made in cash. We pulled in over $10,000 that night.

I decided that since my employees were not on the clock and would not get paid for what they did I would split the money between the company and my employees. I mean if we did not sell the food most of it would have been spoiled for lack of refrigeration.

With that said, I gave each porter $500 each and I gave the family that helped me $1,000 and $2,000 to Paula for a total of $5,000. The remainder of $5,000 went to my employer Host International, who got their money back and more since I charged double and sometimes triple what the company selling price was. I mean hey it's been 46 years since the blackout of 1977 so sue me.

By the time Paula and I left the airport I had put in a 28-hour shift, tired and burned out, Paula drove us to her parents' summer cottage in Vermont for some well-deserved rest and relaxation.

My Girlfriend Paula

As I mentioned I was dating a girl named Paula, she was four years younger than me, about 5'4 blond, green eyes and very attractive. We met at our annual Host International Christmas party and really hit it off.

Paula was adopted when she was very young by a German Jewish family. She was Italian by birth but raised in the Jewish tradition. Soon after we started dating, we moved into an apartment in Kew Gardens, in Queens New York. The apartment was close to the airport, her college, and her parents so it worked fine for us.

She was a design major at Queens College and a good one. When Host International was thinking of redesigning one of their food units I was able to get the General Manager to look at her work and he agreed to give her a chance to do the design.

It was a happy time for me. I enjoyed my job, had a great girlfriend and was making good money. When you are young you can work all day and party all night and never feel the effects. I often went two or three days straight with little or no sleep. I mean we would work all day and party all night.

Like most employees at the airport Paula and I would go to after-hours parties, mostly with people from work. One night we went to this after-hours party given by one of the cashiers named Christine, she was an attractive chubby girl with blond hair and big tits.

Many of the people were doing prescription drugs and smoking weed, including Paula. Drugs, however, were not my thing so I did not take any.

Christine sits next to me and hands me a Jack Daniels and the next thing I know we are in her bedroom on her bed, and she is naked on top of me trying to pull my pants down.

Luckily Paula came into the bedroom looking for me at just the right time and got her off me. I got dressed and left. Christine had put a Quaalude in my drink which made me drowsy and increased my sexual arousal at the same time.

Paula and I stayed together well after I left the airport and moved into an apartment in the village on west fourth street in Manhattan, New York. Life was great but it would be drugs that would change our relationship.

While she was the love of my life, she was paranoid from the drugs. I remember one time we had just moved out of the Kew Gardens apartment and into the apartment in the village. Her friend josh then moved into our Kew Gardens apartment. The first week he was there a tenant who lived downstairs went to Josh's apartment and put three bullets in his chest. Why, because Josh was playing his music too loud.

Paranoid from prescription drugs Paula was afraid that the tenant was going to come to our village apartment and shoot us. It was a big deal at the time, as it made the news on CBS Television.

Paula's drug use continued to get worse and unfortunately, she was addicted to prescription drugs, especially quaaludes and after two years of bringing her to St. Vincents Hospital to get her stomach pumped, we broke up. Sadly, she died of an overdose on December 15, 1991, in our village apartment in Manhattan.

Anthony Perkins

Eventually I stayed longer at the United terminal which had a great restaurant and large bar and the United Airlines Private Lounge reserved for the rich and powerful.

Working at the airport I met many celebrities, people like rock and Roll legend Chuck Berry and blues guitarists Johnny and Edgar Winters but the celebrity that had the biggest impact on me was Anthony Perkins from the movie "Psycho"

I was introduced to Anthony Perkins by my bartender who tendered bar in the United Terminal Private lounge.

Mr. Perkins was with his family, so I met his wife Berinthia "Berry" Berenson, the younger sister of actress Marisa Berenson and their boys Oz and Elvis.

They were very nice, and Mr. Perkins talked with me for about 30 minutes while his family sat in the lounge waiting for their flight. Believe it or not we had a lot in common, we were both born in Manhattan, New York and we were both big Elvis Presley fans. I mean he named his boy Elvis for God's sake.

We drank scotch and bourbon and talked about Elvis records and Elvis's movies. As we drank and talked, Mr. Perkins told me that he was offered the starring role in the movie "King Creole "but turned it down. The role went to Elvis Presley.

Over the years, I would drink and talk with Anthony Perkins whenever he came through the United Airlines Private lounge. I found Mr. Perkins to be a gentle, polite, intelligent man that I liked very much and was very saddened when Anthony Perkins passed away of AIDS on September 12, 1992, at age 60.

Ironically his wife Berry Berenson would die on September 11ᵗʰ, 2001, in the World Trade Center attacks when a highbacked plane crashed into the World Trade Center which I witnessed firsthand from where I worked just five short blocks away

Lufthansa Heist

In the 1970's JFK International airport was a hotbed of crime. I mean you could get almost anything you wanted. Guys who worked in the cargo area at JFK would tell me that if I needed a television or a stereo or jewelry for my girlfriend, they could get it and for a fraction of the cost. Why? Because they would steal it!

I have an original Salvatore Dahi etching that my mother gave me years ago. Apparently, it came from a JFK heist. My family on my mother's side is well connected, but that's another story and another book.

Anyway, the food service company that I worked for, Host International, ran all the bars in the International arrivals building and one bar was the Lufthansa bar. It was a posh bar and one that I would stop in towards the end of my shift and kibbitz with the bartender Franz. The bar usually closes at 9:00 pm but would stay open later if there were planes arriving late from Germany. On this night, December 11, 1978, Lufthansa had two planes delayed and we were contracted to stay open until 2:00 am So I got the privilege of closing the Lufthansa bar which I did promptly at 2:00 am.

My car was parked in employee lot 12 just minutes from Lufthansa Cargo. I drove home and went to sleep and was awakened at 5:30 am by the opening manager who informed me that some of the gates at the bars in the International arrivals building were banged in apparently someone tried to break in.

I called my friend John, head of security for the Port Authority of New York who then informed me about the Lufthansa heist and that all hell had broken out at the airport.

The Lufthansa heist was the largest cash robbery committed on American soil at the time. The money and jewelry have never been recovered and the heist was one of the longest-investigated crimes in U.S. history

At the airport John gave me the rundown and I found out that my friend Rudi Eirich, the night shift cargo traffic manager was taken hostage along with John Murray, a senior cargo agent who I had met with Rudi was also taken hostage. Sometimes after work the three of us would go to the Airline 'diner in Astoria queens for an early breakfast.

In the movie" Goodfellows" they position the Airline Diner more near JFK International airport, but the diner is more towards LaGuardia airport than JFK.

Airline Diner

Apparently, the attempted break in of the Host International bars was just a rouse to draw attention away from the Lufthansa heist. All in all, the heist netted almost six million dollars which was never recovered.

When I saw the movie "Goodfellas, the Lufthansa heist scene brought back a lot of real memories as it

Lufthansa Heist

was a pretty accurate representation of the event, except for not showing the attempted break-ins of the bars at the international arrivals building.

Of course, in the movie Morris Kessler (Morrie) the wig guy did not exist, the real information came from Louis Werner who told bookmaker Martin Krugman who in turn told Jimmy Burke and the rest is history

A Crash Course in Stealing

The rule of thumb in the hospitality industry is that most bartenders steal. That's just the way it is, and the rule of thumb is to allow the bartender to steal 10 percent of the sales, any more means that bartender must go.

So, you may ask yourself how does a bartender steal? There are several ways a bartender can steal, however in this case the methods of stealing are specific to Host International and airport operations.

At JFK airport they used an automated liquor system that dispensed alcohol and automatically rang that alcohol sale in the register. Foolproof right! – Wrong!

The liquor bottles were in a locked room behind the bar and were connected to the automated liquor system using plastic tubing connected to the bottles and then to a button under the bar. A different button for each type of alcohol. Such as a button for Gin, Vodka, Rum and so on. Basically, these were the well brands, the top shelf liquor were still poured by hand.

There is also a cocktail button for each liquor under the bar as well. Usually, a shot is one ounce of liquor, and a cocktail button is 1-1/2 ounces of liquor.

Okay let's beat the automated liquor system and steal a few bucks.

If someone orders a Bloody Mary, Vodka, and tomato juice mixer, give the customer no alcohol at all. Since vodka is tasteless, just float dry vermouth on top of the drink and the customer will most likely tell the bartender that the drink is too strong. Pocket the money. Easy Peasy!

Another way is to take a slip straw, the one that the bartender puts in your drink and just stick it up the dispenser spout by the alcohol button. Since this automated system is connected by hoses to the liquor bottles in the back there is air lock thus by using a straw you can break that air lock and the liquor pours out. Put one, two or more glasses under the bar and have the liquor pour into these glasses and now you have alcohol you don't have to ring up. Easy Peasy!

But the best way to beat the system and the way most dishonest bartenders try to steal is to bring in their own bottle. If done right, a bartender can go into business for him or herself and become an entrepreneur at your expense.

This principle works best with management trainees or lazy managers that do not want to do the work. The work I'm referring to is inventory. It is imperative to take an inventory at the close of each shift. A naïve manager or a lazy manager will let the bartender take the nightly inventory. That inventory is then matched against a par system (the amount to always keep on hand).

For example, say the par for Absolute vodka is four bottles and the bar has three bottles then management needs to order 1 bottle.

So, here's the scam: The bartender brings in his own bottle of Absolute vodka and when he takes inventory, he finds that the bar has three full bottles and based on par, the bar needs to order one bottle to make the par, but the bartender adds his empty bottle and has management order two bottles of vodka.

So, every time the bartender's bottle is empty, he hands his empty bottle in for a new bottle and for a one-time investment of say twenty-five dollars, the bartender is in business for himself using his bottle instead of the bar's bottle of vodka.

For example, he or she will split sales, one from the bar and one from his or her bottle until the bottle is empty. Keep in mind that a litter of Vodka contains 33.8 ounces. So, using the standard of one ounce of alcohol per drink, you can get 30 drinks per bottle.

If each drink sells for $10.00 then the bartender can expect to make $300.00 per night from his bottle. Money the bar loses nightly.

You might ask yourself well what if someone else decides to take inventory? Well, then the bartender just breaks his or her bottle and discards the bottle in the garbage leaving the correct par amount of four bottles at the bar. Easy Peasy!

Ah, but what about the money the bartender did not ring up? You just can't put the stolen money in your pocket? Well, you can but you run a very good chance of getting caught. So, to be a good thief takes some planning.

Let us look at some common methods of accounting for the money a bartender has stolen.

How To Steal One Hundred Dollars a Day

This is easy at the bar. A good thief uses what is around him to steal. Most people have what's called tunnel vision, that is they only see what is right in front of them. A smart dishonest bartender knows that and will use the customer or manager's tunnel vision to their advantage.

A good professional thief must have an accounting method to keep track of how much they have stolen. There are two main methods that most dishonest bartenders use: The straw method or the loose coin method or both.

Straw Method

Every bar has sip straws, you know these short blue or red plastic straws at the bar. You order a drink, and the bartender puts a sip straw in your drink. Well, they make great tools for counting.

Say you want to steal $100.00 per day and the average cost of a drink back then is $5.00. To count how much you have stolen for the day you take one blue sip straw and put into the red sip straws, when you have 20 blue sip straws in with the red sip straws you have successfully stolen $100.00.

Okay, too obvious for you, then use the loose coin method. A simple method by which the bartender uses loose coins to add up how much money he has stolen.

Loose Coin Method

In a cash register draw you have change sections or coin slots divided into 5 sections with each section broken into pennies, nickels, dimes, quarters and one empty coin slot. The empty slot is the one to watch.

The way it works is that every time you steal five dollars you put a nickel in the empty coin slot signifying the 5 dollars you stole, ten dollars is a dime, and a quarter represents 25 dollars. So, if you see that empty coin slot with change and you see 3 quarters and 2 dimes and 1 nickel that bartender has stolen one hundred dollars. Of course, any combination will work.

As a manager the best way to deter this and really screw up the bartenders is to walk behind the bar, open the cash drawer and jumble up all those coins in the empty coin slot by putting the coins back in their proper coin slots, you know quarters with quarters and dimes with dimes and so on. This will screw up a dishonest bartender's counting system and make him sweat.

Of course, once you have stolen the money you need to get it out of the restaurant as quickly as possible and there are two main methods that a good thief will use. Either the short drawer method or the friend method. I said smart thief because many thieves are not so smart and easily caught. I will discuss these other methods later in this chapter.

Short Drawer Method

At the beginning of his shift a bartender is given a cash drawer commonly called a bank, containing the amount of money he needs to work with for the day, usually two hundred dollars. This bank is used to make change and perform daily transactions.

At the end of the shift the cash drawer is counted and should contain the correct sales according to the register reading and the two-hundred-dollar bank that the bartender started with.

In the short drawer method, the bartender takes out the one hundred dollars he wants to steal leaving the drawer short, with only a one hundred bank and builds the stolen money back using one of the accounting methods mentioned above.

The Friend Method

Most experienced managers have a store policy that they do not want friends of the bartender hanging around the bar or for that matter employees whose shift has ended. Why? Because the bartender may give free drinks to their friends and coworkers, and this becomes an excellent vehicle to get the stolen money out of the restaurant.

So, it is simple, a friend of the bartender orders a drink, gives a twenty-dollar bill to the bartender, and gets one hundred and twenty dollars back in change and leaves. The money has left the building. Easy Peasy.

However, some dishonest bartenders are not so smart I had one female bartender who would stuff the money she stole in her bra. At the beginning of her shift, she was a 34B, at the end of her shift she was a 34D. I mean you could see the twenty-dollar bills hanging out of her bra like she was a stripper working the pole at a topless club, not too smart.

Another female bartender would wear and wig and stuff the money in the wig. I mean one day she had twenty-dollar bills coming out of her head – not so smart.

And then I had a bartender who had a note pad stuffed in his back pants. He would write down every drink he did not ring up and was stuffing ten- and twenty-dollar bills down his crotch. When we had security search him, we found three hundred dollars in his crotch.

I asked him "If you were a manager and you found a guy writing down sales in a note pad and you found three hundred dollars in his crotch what would you do?"

He says to me "I guess I would fire him"

I said, "Yea me too" Not too smart.

Cocktail Waitresses are no different. They steal as well. Back then the cocktail waitresses wore skimpy outfits like the Playboy Club bunnies did, only no bunny tail. They were sexy and got great tips, however some waitresses just had to steal.

JFK International Airport is a transient place, people come and go, and most people will never come back, so you really don't get repeat business. So, with regards to bars and cocktail waitresses a good management practice is to make sure every customer gets a bill. It's not only good for the customer but a control tool for management. Every drink at every table should have a bill and then a receipt after the bill has been paid.

Sounds simple, but which bill does the customer get? I know you are saying to yourself "what do you mean which bill?"

Did you ever go to a bar or to a restaurant and get the wrong bill? Was that bill less than you thought it was going to be? Did you say to the waitress "Hey this bill is less than my bill should be? Let me tell the waitress I should be paying more than the bill she gave me?"

Most people, if they got a bill less than what they owed, would keep their mouth shut, pay it, and maybe leave a larger tip. This is exactly what a dishonest cocktail waitress or waiter for that matter is counting on.

You see when a customer pays cash for his bill, gets his change, and leaves his bill on the table, the waitress picks up that bill and puts it in her change purse

Throughout the evening every time a customer pays cash and leaves the bill, the waitress picks up the bill and puts it in her change purse

Within a short period of time, the waitress will have several bills to choose from. So, when she sees a customer take out cash to pay, she finds a bill that is close to the customer's bill and drops it on the table, collects the money and puts the money in her change purse and no sale has rung up. Easy Peasy.

I mentioned before that all the alcohol in airport operations are on an automated system, except for top shelf liquor, however, bottle beer and wine by the glass is not.

These two items bottled beer and wines by the glass pose the biggest problem for stealing as they are hard to control and dishonest bartenders and or waitresses know this. So, management needs to count, and I mean count every empty beer bottle. Company policy should dictate that the waitress or bartender must return all empty beer bottles back to the bar and put the "empties" back into the boxes they came in. A case of beer contains 24 bottles of beer so if a bar has three cases of empty beer bottles and 10 loose empty beer bottles, they should have sales for 82 bottles of beer. When management closes out the bar register the amount of bottled beer sold will show on the menu item report and should match the physical count of actual empties. If not, you have a thief.

Wine by the glass is a little more difficult because depending on who is pouring the number of glasses served per bottle may vary. For example, a liter of wine contains 33.8 ounces of wine, if the bar or restaurant serves a six-ounce glass of wine, they should get approximately five glasses of wine per bottle. So, it is parament that management runs an item report and compares the empty wine bottles with the actual wine sales by the glass.

The Trattoria Restaurant

I am working as the manager of the Trattoria restaurant, an Italian American restaurant in the then called Pan Am Building, now the Met Life building on 45th street in New York City.

Pan Am Building

The restaurant was part of Restaurant Associates, a restaurant management company that during the 1970s had operated such theme restaurants as Mama Leone's, Ma Bell and the world-famous Taven on the Green which was later sold to former President Donald Trump.

It was a huge restaurant with indoor and outdoor seating and a long bar that easily seated over 25 people. It was a tablecloth restaurant, complete with professional waiters, bus boys, a maître d, and a real Italian Chef. The Trattoria restaurant also had a large cocktail area complete with cocktail waitresses and New York bartenders. I say New York bartenders because back then you needed a bartender who could make lots of drinks in a very short period and handle the large crowd during rush hour. That's a New York bartender.

The food was some of the best Italian American cuisine I have ever tasted in public, and the desserts were to die for. Our Pastry Chef was from Germany. He was unbelievable. He would come to work around midnight to make his desserts and he was gone by seven am. In all the years I worked at the Trattoria; I have only seen him once as he left in passing at the end of his shift. Anyway, his cheesecake, and Zuppa Inglese was the best I have ever tasted to this day.

The restaurant Chef was straight from Italy, spoke little English and was a tyrant in the kitchen. I remember one time one of the floor managers came into the kitchen and told the Chef that he is taking too long to put out the food orders and to hurry it up customers are waiting.

The Chef looked at him and took an 8-inch frying pan from the utilities shelf and bopped him over the head and knocked him out. Then he screamed for me and in broken English asked me keep these "assholes" out of his kitchen. I had one of the porters remove the floor manager from the kitchen floor and service continued as if nothing had happened.

Let me give you one of the first rules of the restaurant business. That is that the restaurant is separated into two parts, the Front Of the House (F.O.H.) and the Back Of the House (B.O.H.).

There is also a chain of command just like in the military. The general manager oversees the entire restaurant, then the manager, assistant managers and finally the floor or dining room manager. In the kitchen the Chef is King, then the Sous chef.

Proper protocol requires you to ask the Chef if you can enter his or her domain. If you don't ask, well you may get a bop on the head from a frying pan. There you go!

Also, it was different in the late seventies, no real employment laws like a hostile workplace or sexual harassment. If you were a female and someone slapped your ass. Okay no big deal go back to work.

As I mentioned the restaurant had a large bar and being in the Pan Am building at around 5 o'clock people would come from work and stop in for drinks before going home, so many times our bar was three or four deep (customers standing and not sitting),

I remember one time, a gentleman walked in and sat at the bar around 4 o'clock and asked the bartender for a glass of water, and said he was waiting for his girlfriend, the bartender gave him a glass of water and went about her business setting up.

As he sat at the bar, he was fidgety and nervous. The bartender asked him if he was okay, and he said yes. A few minutes later he began to bang the bar with his fists commenting that his girlfriend was late. She called the floor manager who told him that if he made another outburst, he would have to leave. He apologized and was quiet. The floor manager told me about the incident, and I said watch that guy you never know.

As the bar started to fill up and get crowded a woman took a seat next to the man with the glass of water and put her handbag around her bar stool and ordered a Whiskey Sour. As she was talking with others at the bar the man who ordered the water got up and in the middle of the aisle dropped kicked the glass and hit a patron square in the forehead, cutting him badly. At that moment he grabbed the handbag from the bar chair from the woman drinking the Whiskey Sour and ran out of the Trattoria into the Pan Am building and was never seen again.

A big mistake on my part and one that I will never make again. Once the patron started banging on the bar, I should have had him removed from the restaurant. Lesson learned

The restaurant business is a tough business with

long hours and working when everyone else is partying, so it is logical that many of the managers and staff hang out together and usually party after hours. I was in my mid-twenties then and I was lucky because the bartenders were mostly women, good looking and a lot of fun.

Restaurant Associates had placed an ad for bartenders and cocktail waitresses for our busy season and for some reason I got a drove of playboy bunnies from the Playboy Club on 59th street coming in for cocktail waitress positions. These were very hot looking women, exuding sex with good waitress experience.

Our cocktail positions at the Trattoria were prime positions, the busy period was from five to eight pm and the restaurant closed at 10 pm, so the hours were great, and the tips were fabulous you could easily make $300.00 to $400.00 a week in tips working just three or four days a week for only three hours per day. That amount is $1200.00 to $1500.00 in today's dollars.

I guess these former Playboy bunnies knew that because during the interview they would tell me that they would do anything to get this job and that we were going to work well together – WOW.

To be honest there was one Playboy Bunny that I was going to hire, she had five years' experience as a cocktail waitress, very attractive and was also number one on my GM's list of hires. But then it happened, that thing you see in movies or read about in books - Kismet!

Denice Johns

This woman walks in wearing the standard waitress uniform white blouse and black pants. She is in heels and stands about 5' 9 inches tall, she is thin, all hair and boobs and has three buttons open on her blouse, so her big boobs are exposed and bends over, so her boobs are almost in my face and says that she is here for the bartender position.

I gave her an application and went about my business. Moments later she comes back and tells me she does not have a pen to fill out the application. I look at her and think to myself what kind of person goes to an interview without a pen, but I decide to give her my solid silver Cross pen to use to fill out the application and continue my management duties.

I say to myself I know this woman from somewhere, then it hits me. I saw her on television, that's right television. I was watching television one afternoon and she is promoting a boxing match with another girl, and I said to myself this is the most attractive woman I had ever seen in my life and believe me I have been with a lot of sexy women. To be honest, in person she is even more attractive.

She comes back hands me her application and it is impressive; she has worked many Italian restaurants as a bartender and a waitress and one in particular: Roma D' Note was a well-known Italian restaurant in Manhattan. She was perfect in every way. She had the looks, personality, and experience.

I tell her that we do not have any bartender positions available but if she wants a cocktail waitress position there is one available. She says yes so, I give her the standard test for a cocktail waitress which is to make a setup.

A setup is a term that means the proper glassware and mixers for different kinds of drinks. I told her get me 1 beer, 1 scotch and soda, 1 bourbon neat and 1 gin and tonic.

As she turns around to leave I say to her "Excuse me what about my Cross Pen."

She smiles and puts her hand in her bra and pulls my pen from her bra. Smiling she says "Sorry" and hands me my pen and leaves to do the setup.

I tell my GM I want to hire her as a cocktail waitress over the Playboy bunny. A heated discussion ensues between me and the GM and after much discussion he agrees that we will hire her.

When I go back to the front of the restaurant this girl is nowhere to be found so I start looking for her and find her in front of the soda machine looking dumbfounded.

I said to her 'It's been almost 15 minutes, aren't you finished yet".

She says "Well you have no tonic water, just quinine water, so I can't compete the setup"

I look at her and smile and I say, "You know every bartender or waitress in this business knows that tonic water and quinine water are one in the same." So did you work at Roma D' Note or was that I lie?"

She then says to me that she did work at Roma D' Note but not as a bartender or a waitress but as a singer.

I say" A singer!" Then she says I'm a fast learner, please give me a shot."

I tell her "Okay, you are hired I'll give you a chance to prove yourself." Of course, this is after I already hired her without her knowledge. I mean this was the woman of my dreams and if she could be a competent cocktail waitress, well I'm not going to let this one get away.

Sufficive to say she was one of the best cocktail waitresses I had. She could easily handle 30 tables without a problem and almost everyone who came into the restaurant (mostly businessmen) wanted to sit in her section. She was very popular. After a while I found out why she was so popular. While she was an exceptional waitress, she was also a woman who knew how to market herself.

For example, before her shift she would splash water on her blouse so her boobs were exposed, and she would go into the kitchen and take appetizers that other waiters ordered off the side (where food is placed after its cooked) and give it to her customers as a complement of the house. All to increase the check and increase her tips. She was a marketing expert in that manner.

It is said that a manager makes over one thousand decisions a day and in hiring Denice, I believe it was the smartest decision in my life because not only was

Denice one of my best waitresses she became my best friend, my cohort in life and finally my wife.

I believe that kismet played a role in her coming into the Trattoria for a job that day because the chances of the women of my dreams that I saw on television applying for a job in the Trattoria is a one in a million chance.

Denice - Johns – Golio in Italy

Later in life Denice became a top ten recording artist under the name of Tara Butler in the United States and in Europe, a studio executive for a motion picture company, a successful real estate broker and an elected politician in the City and State of New York. I really lucked out in marrying her.

Many actors and singers and entertainers enter the restaurant field as bartenders or waiters, and you ask them what they do for a living, many say that they are actors or entertainers and then you ask them how long they have been a waiter or a bartender.

When they tell you that they have been a bartender or a waiter for more than 5 years, they are not just actors, entertainers, or singers but hospitality workers with a dream. Of course, Denice was the exception because she was all the above.

Back then many of the staff dated, a practice that is not an accepted management practice. Anyway, the General Manager was dating a blond who had come from the Midwest to the big city of New York. She was tall, thin, and attractive with no experience in the restaurant industry.

The General Manager asked me to make her a cocktail waitress, so I did. She was so bad at her job that I told the GM that she is terrible and that the other cocktail waitresses are complaining about her.

So, the General Manager says "Yea I know, but she is my girlfriend so is there any way we can keep her?" I said to him alright I'll figure something out. So, I cut her down to just two tables figuring she could handle that. I was wrong.

She got poor tips from giving poor service, my GM said I going to have the waiters and cocktail waitresses pool tips that way she could make some money.

Bad idea, the front of the house was against it and began to protest the idea of pooling tips, so the idea was abandoned, and my GM had to fire his girlfriend.

Later I found out that she got a job as a hostess in a small restaurant and was dating the owner and his son to keep her job – There you go!

Biltmore and Roosevelt Hotels

When I left the Trattoria restaurant, I interviewed for the Food and Beverage Controller position at the World-Famous Biltmore and Roosevelt Hotels in New York City.

Biltmore Hotel

While I had a lot of food and beverage experience with multi-unit foodservice, the only tablecloth restaurant experience I had was at the trattoria restaurant, so this was going to be kind of new to me.

The Biltmore Hotel was a luxury hotel at 335 Madison Avenue in Midtown Manhattan, New York City, and the Roosevelt Hotel at 45 East 45th Street between Madison and Vanderbilt avenues. Both hotels were developed by the New York Central Railroad and the New York, New Haven, and Hartford Railroad.

These hotels had secret passageways that led to Grand Central Station and each other so you could travel from one hotel to the other underground and never be seen.

The Biltmore hotel was that hotel where countless couples would meet their dates "Under the Biltmore Clock" and the author J. D. Salinger frequently met William Shawn, the editor of *The New Yorker* in the Biltmore's lobby under the Biltmore clock. J. D. Salinger would go on to write about the Biltmore Hotel in his book "The Catcher in The Rye." It was also a meeting place for Writer F. Scott

Fitzgerald who also met under the clock at the Biltmore.

I interviewed with the Director of Food and Beverage at the time which went well and as we talked, he said "I see you graduated from New York Technical College in Brooklyn, New York." We are alumni, that's my college as well."

The conversation then changed to professors at the school like Professor McHugh who taught dining room management or Professor Veal who taught culinary arts.

He offered me the position and I took it and started my journey in the hotel business as a Food and Beverage Controller. My responsibilities were to compile and calculate the costs of food and beverage sold and using cashier records and other summaries determine sales and profit, as well as calculate menu prices and so forth. Main areas of responsibility are calculating profit and loss for all food and beverage operations in the hotel and recording data to keep perpetual inventory.

It was okay at first, I mean I was given my own office and could make my own hours. The key here was to have all my paperwork done on time and be available for meeting at a moment's notice.

My day started with breakfast in the Palm Court, a room with marble walls and bronze decorations. In the center of the room was a gilded clock with a pair of sculpted nude figures. This was the "Under the Biltmore Clock." The Palm court had a skylight and of course palm trees, thus the name Palm court.

I sat with the Director of Food and Beverage and the General Manager of the Hotel, and we had breakfast. White glove service on bone China. I usually had a croissant and a cup of coffee, but you could have anything from pancakes to Eggs Benedict.

After I went to my office or to the kitchens to do inventories and complete my paperwork.

At that time, I was employed by Realty Hotels Inc, which was a holding company that owned the hotels, as well as the management company for the Biltmore, Commodore, and Roosevelt hotels.

The hotels operated what is called a "Brigade de cuisine" a structured team of individual stations developed by the famous French Chef Auguste Escoffier.

The hotels had very large kitchens with several floors having finishing kitchens throughout the hotel. A finishing kitchen is a small kitchen that receives prepared foods for reheating, assembling, portioning, and serving.

At the back of the house, the staff were all union workers and only worked in their specific position.

For example, the fry cook was responsible for only fried foods and did not work at the grill station. Following the Brigade de cuisine" the hotels had the following kitchen staff:

- Chef
- Sous-Chef
- Cuisinier (Cook)
- Saucier (Sauce Cook)
- Commis (Assistant Cook)
- Rôtisseur (Roast Cook)
- Grillardin (Grill Cook)
- Friturier (Fry Cook)
- Poissonnier (Fish Cook)
- Potager (Soup Cook)
- Legumier (Vegetable cook)
- Plongeur (Dishwasher or Kitchen Porter)
- Marmiton (Pot and Pan Washer)

Eventually, I moved up to the Food and Beverage Director position and was responsible for ensuring the quality of food and service while maintaining overall guest satisfaction with their dining experience. Menu development, profit, and loss analysis as well as the hiring, firing, training and the supervision of front of the house staff.

Most of the front of the house staff was male, in their fifties and union workers. They received excellent hourly wages and tips at the Biltmore and Roosevelt hotels so stealing was at a minimum in the front of the house.

For example, Mario was the Maître d' Hotel of the Palm Court at the Biltmore Hotel. The Maître is responsible for greeting guests, seating them, and taking care of their needs during their dining experience. At the end of our lunch period Mario had made so much money in tips that he had to take a break and deposit his tips in the bank, I mean his pockets were literally bursting with cash.

However, it was not the same in the back of the house. Food cost was up, and the Chef was missing food, mainly meats such as legs of Veal and Legs of lamb. It was hard to figure out how this was happening since we followed the standard practice of keeping all food and beverage locked.

To get food for service the Chef or the Sous Chef had to requisition that food, sign for it and then the storage areas were once again locked.

So, we were unable to figure out how food was being stolen. I installed a hidden camera in the storage area and after reviewing the footage I could not believe what I saw.

The night crew would bring a ladder in to work to the garbage area and climb over the tall, locked gate to the storage area, then using a hammer and a screwdriver they would knock out the bolts that held the hinges of the walk-in refrigerator door and then remove the door.

Once in the walk-in refrigerator they would steal legs of Veal and Lamb and sometimes 10-pound bags of chopped meat and put the stolen meat into garbage bags. Then throw the garbage bags into the garbage bin in the back of the restaurant.

At the end of their shift, they would retrieve the garbage bags with the stolen meat and go about their business.

The Roosevelt Hotel

The Roosevelt hotel was named for Theodore Roosevelt, the former president of the United States and was equally impressive. The hotel's "Grill Room was the starting place for a young "Lawarence Welk" to begin his climb to fame and it is where for many years Guy Lombardo and his band brought in the New Year on New Years Eve.

In 1952, President Eisenhower had his campaign offices in the Roosevelt hotel and the hotel can be seen in many movies. The ballroom scene in "Wall Street" was shot inside the ballroom of the Roosevelt Hotel and the films "Boiler Room, the French Connection, Malcolm X, and Maid in Manhattan" were all partially filmed in the hotel.

By 1978, The Roosevelt hotel was leased to the to Pakistan International Airlines (PIA) and no longer my responsibility. Under PIA airlines sales began to decrease. Infusions of cash by Prince Faisal bin Khalid bin Abdulaziz Al Saud kept the Roosevelt

Hotel a float for a period but poor sales and the COVID 19 epidemic closed its doors.

Roosevelt Hotel

In 2023, The hotel reopened only to become a shelter for asylum seekers.

Commodore Hotel

Due to declining profits, the Commodore Hotel closed on May 18, 1976, and Realty Hotels Inc. sold the hotel to the Trump and Hyatt corporations who offered to take over the Commodore and renovate it into the Grand Hyatt hotel.

Commodore Hotel

Under the Trump organization, construction commenced from 1978- 1980 and as is with most Trump properties he removed or destroyed nearly all the Commodore's landmark decorations to replace them with new cheaper ones.

The partnership between Trump and Hyatt, fell apart and Hyatt, acquired Trump's stake in the hotel in 1996. Due to declining profits the Hyatt Grand Central is scheduled to close permanently sometime after 2023.

The writing was on the wall it was obvious to me that the Biltmore was next on the list to close, so I needed to make some extra money fast.

Adam & Eve and the Living Room

Adam and Eve was located at 141 East 45th Street in a brownstone just a few blocks from the Biltmore so it was perfect and the Living Room, another brownstone type was located at 151 East 49th Street. So, they were both only a few blocks from the Biltmore Hotel

In most topless bars in the late 1970's and early 1980's nearly all transactions were done in cash. I mean drinks were purchased in cash, the topless dancers were paid in cash and of course all the tips to the topless dancers received were in cash so you could say that a topless bar is a cash business.

Adam and Eve and the Living Room

That's where I come in; I am going to work as a floor manager and see if I can spot and catch those employees who are stealing. Both locations had long bars that easily seated twenty-five or more patrons and when you add the patrons that are standing at the bar, which could be two or three deep there could be seventy-five patrons at the bar, drinking and waving money at the topless dancers.

Both Adam and Eve and the Living room had 50 tables all crunched together where patrons and the topless dancers would sit.

Abe, a Jewish guy in his late forties who I believed owned both the Adam and Eve and the Living Room topless clubs says to me "Listen Dan, see if you can get the girls to sell more alcohol while you are looking for the low life's that are stealing from me."

"Okay Abe, I'll see what I can do." I tell him

I know the deal, Abe wants to sell overpriced cheap liquor, watered-down drinks and watered-down wine and get the biggest bang for his buck.

So, one day I say" Hey Abe come here, I want to show you something" As he looks, I take out a half-bottle of "Pol Roger Champagne" it is a cheap brand of French Champagne and pour him a glass and ask him to taste it.

"Okay he says its cheap champagne so what"

"Well, it's not champagne." I told Abe.

" What?" Abe says.

I tell him it is a combination of white wine, salt, sugar and ginger ale and costs less than two dollars to make and the topless dancers can sell it for $50.00 per bottle.

Abe loves the idea and tells the dancers to push the champagne. The way it works is that when a topless dancer is sitting with a guy, the dancer will ask the guy if he is going to buy her a drink. The guy almost always say of course, whatever you want.

She then says "I want Champagne"

While the guy is looking at her breasts and being fondled, the bartender pulls a bottle of the made-up stuff from the ice with the cork already pulled and pours the champagne. An easy fifty bucks.

Watching the bartenders at the topless clubs I notice that a regular would come to the bar and put a twenty-dollar bill on the bar, the bartender would take his order and say the customer orders draft beer for $5.00, keeping the twenty-dollar bill on the bar, the customer would continue to order drinks all night.

When the customer is ready to leave, the bartender takes the twenty-dollar bill and only rings up the draft beer for $5.00 and gives the customer change of $15.00, where then the customer then leaves the change as a tip for the bartender who puts it in his tip cup

Disco Meats

Abe knew I was the Food and Beverage Director of the Biltmore and tells me his friend has a meat company called "Disco Meats "and I can get a great price on meat. So, I set it up with the Purchasing Director of the hotel to place an order with Disco Meats.

On that Wednesday we are expecting a meat delivery from Disco Meats. It never comes, so I call Bobby at Disco Meats and ask him where the delivery is.

"Hey bobby where is my delivery" I say.

"Dan, we could not get a truck today" "So most likely you will get your delivery on Thursday or at the latest on Friday' he says.

"You guys don't have any trucks? I ask him

"Well yea, we highjack the trucks from other meat companies, didn't Abe tell you" Bobby says.

"Really I must have missed that part thanks Bobby" I say and hang up.

Sufficive to say I got my meat delivery on that Friday, but I never ordered from them again.

The next week I am home watching CBS News and the News flash is "Gangland Hit on East 45th Street."

I see a guy with a briefcase lying face down on the sidewalk. The news commentator says the police found one million dollars in the brief case and they believe it was a mob hit because the guy was shot three times; two times in the chest and one time in the head.

Then they flash his name over the television: Abe Burnstein, who ran topless clubs for the Gambino crime family. I quit that part-time job the next day.

Adams Apple

With the Biltmore hotel's future uncertain I land a part-time position at one of the world-famous Discos of the 1980s "Adams Apple" located on 61st and 1st Avenue in New York City.

Adams Apple

I was hired by one of the owners, Joe Cavallaro who was one of the producers of the musical "Hair" and in the mid-sixties, Joe Cavallaro was the general manager of the Cheetah club on 53rd Street and Broadway which helped Jimi Hendrix career take off.

I was hired to help the disco club sell more premium wine. I am certified from both the French and German wine Council, so I know a thing or two about wine.

Apparently, Adams Apple had an extensive wine cellar and wanted to sell more wine and Champagne to increase the average check of the restaurant portion of the club.

Sounds easy, but the menu consisted mainly of hamburgers, fried chicken and the like. However, a Beaujolais goes well with a hamburger and fries and a German Resling Kabinett is a great accompaniment to fried chicken. See my book "The Fundamentals of Wine" available at Barnes and Noble to learn more about wine appreciation.

Of course, for me and my wife, we enjoy a nice bottle of Prosecco with fried chicken and caviar – out of this world!

The club itself was almost always crowded nightly and at the bar, guys and girls were eyeing each other looking for a hookup. Adams Apple was the first real disco and pick-up bar in Manhattan. The club had matchbooks with a space inside for names and phone numbers, two mirrored dance floors and lots of palm trees, real and fake. The bar was crammed with hungry guys looking for hot girls.

Adams Apple Matchbook

The two suspended dance floors were packed like sardines with sexy people dancing. The restaurant portion of the club, the forty seats downstairs and the 75 seats upstairs where dinner was served was also full. Wine sales, however, was another story. So being able to increase the average check by getting the waiters to sell a bottle of overpriced wine to their table was a major plus.

After I finish work at the Biltmore Hotel I will go to work at Adams Apple. I worked from 5 pm to 1 am three nights a week, usually Wednesday, Thursday and Saturday nights. I would work as a floor manager and instruct the waiters on the wines Adams Apple wanted to sell that evening. After a while, the job got boring and tedious, except for a few celebrities I would see like radio and TV personality Wolf Man Jack who hosted the TV show "The Midnight Special for CBS television or the actor Lee Marvin, star of the movies: The Dirty Dozen, The Killers, The Professionals, and many others. I was bored and the long hours of working at the Biltmore Hotel and Adams Apple was taking its toll on me.

Adams Apple was positioned directly across the street from the late Comedian Rodney Dangerfield's club "Dangerfield's" and it was not unusual back then to see Rodney Dangerfield in the street and in Adams Apple once in a while.

Sometimes after work I would go to Dangerfield's for a drink or to watch Mr. Dangerfield's show. He knew my face from the club, and we would nod to each other, but he didn't know me.

On one occasion my dad's brothers were in town and I decided to take them to Dangerfield's to see his show. My dad's brothers were all dressed in black or grey Sharkskin suits, the kind the mafia wore in the late 1960's and early 1970's.

Rodney Dangerfield saw me sitting at their table, and knowing my face as the guy he would nod to he began wise cracking our table.

"Look over there, there is the money table" These guys I tell you, look at those suits, I mean these guys look like extras from the movie the Godfather" Rodney says.

I laugh, my dad laughs the audience laughs all laugh except my dad's brothers. Their faces were stoic.

Rodney looks at them and says" I'm Telling you" I get no respect"

The audience laughs,

Look at these guys." Rodney says" If I don't have a good show tonight, I'm going to wind up like Jimmy Hoffa"

The rest of the night was great, and I had a great time despite my dad's stoic brothers.

The first week of working at Adams Apple I met a guy named Jack, he is one of the floor managers and the inventory guy at Adams Apple.

We got to talk and within a short time I quit Adams Apple and took Jack back with me to the Biltmore Hotel and got him the position of Food and Beverage Storeroom Manager. The job as storeroom manager lasted only a short time because within six months the Biltmore Hotel was about to close.

The Biltmore Hotel Closes

After 68 years of the one of the hubs of New York City, the Biltmore abruptly closes on August 14, 1981, two weeks before it had been scheduled to close. Guests were informed that the hotel was closing, and permanent residents were given 30 days to leave.

Demolition crews entered and began destroying the building. The Biltmore's famous clock was rushed out of the Palm Court and parts of the Biltmore were partitioned off for the demolition.

Nearly all the Palm Court and the Madison Room had been reduced to unrecognizable rubble. Walls had been stripped of decoration and piles of plaster lay on the floor. On Vanderbilt Avenue you could see the once grandeur French doors, and ornate bronze fixtures scattered on the sidewalk or in dump trucks ready to be taken away.

Hotel operations were ongoing that day as the hotel was being demolished. I still had food and beverage operations to run for that day but later that day guests were informed in a brief letter that all dining services had ended. Only housekeeping serves remained active as other departments were closed, and employees tried to take whatever memorabilia of the Biltmore Hotel they could before leaving the building.

Employees who came to work that day were let go and told the Biltmore had closed. Employees who were on vacation would come back to find the hotel closed and out of work.

Permanent residents who had only thirty days to vacate their apartments were concerned they would wind up on the street because thirty days was not enough time to move and find another place to live.

It was like a bad dream, but for me it was a living nightmare. Why? Because me and my staff had to secure all the food and beverage and transport it to the other hotel the that the Milstein organization owned - The Milford Plaza

The main problem was to get the food but especially the liquor from the storage area to the trucks and then from the trucks into the storage facilities at the Milford Plaza Hotel.

I needed to personally check each box before it was put on a truck. Liquor boxes contained twelve bottles of liquor per box and were packed in the storage room, then sent up the line to the loading dock and into the trucks.

However, many boxes that were sent to the trucks for delivery were empty, as someone in the line would empty the boxes, steal the liquor, then reclose the boxes and send these empty boxes to the trucks.

Once at the Milford Plaza you needed to do the same thing and the liquor would disappear. I mean, the employees working knew that they would be out of a job in a week, so they had nothing to lose.

The Milford Plaza

The Milstein organization purchased the old Royal Manhattan hotel in 1978, fixed it up and renamed it the Milford Plaza. The hotel opened in 1980 and was ready to take the remains of the Biltmore Hotel.

The Milford Plaza was a low-end hotel with rooms priced at $39 a night. It was located at 700 Eighth Avenue, between 44th and 45th Streets. A seedy area full of porn shops, topless dancing, prostitution, and drugs.

The Milstein organization was not going to operate any of the food and beverage service at the hotel. Room service was to be run by Restaurant Associates and the main restaurants to owned and operated by Mr. Joe Kipness owner of Joe's Pier 52 at 163 West 52d Street and the Hawaii Kai restaurant.

As a side note the Hawaii Kai restaurant was the restaurant used for the "Bamboo Restaurant" that was torched in the movie "Goodfellows."

At the Milford Plaza, Joe Kipness opened the Stagedoor Canteen and Kippys Pier 44, a seafood restaurant fashioned after Joe's Pier 52.

Manhattan Parties

While the Biltmore hotel had a banquet department, as Director of Food and Beverage of the hotel I received a lot of inquiries for catered events as well, which I usually turned over to the banquet department.

However, the Biltmore was closing, and not taking on any new banquets, Jack and I decided to start our own high end catering company. I mean we had lots of potential high-end customers from Biltmore and rather than refer these potential customers to someone else why not refer them to our company.

Also, there were several Sous chefs and wait staff who will be out of work soon, so it was like having a ready-made staff available to work.

After a little research I was able to find a great many event locations that had full kitchens and that solved our major problem so with all concerns resolved we were on our way.

We had an answering service that we paid monthly that would answer our phone number:

"Manhattan Parties" can I help you   No Mr. Golio is out of the office right now; please give me your number and I will have him call you when he returns."

Back then cell phones were a thing of the future, and the big thing was a "pager or a beeper" which is a wireless telecommunications device that receives and displays a message and you had to go to a pay phone and call the person back.

Just like many Real Estate Brokers and agents, we met our clients at the rental location so there was no need for an actual office. We acquired a suite number from Mailbox etc. for our mail. A suite number by the way is more upscale than a box number.

Through contacts and word of mouth advertising Manhattan Parties planned events for Cover Girl Makeup, Petrossian Caviar NYC, the Bank of Italy, WBLS Radio in New York, the Ford Modeling Agency countless television commercials and music videos and for the CBS television show "Entertainment Tonight."

Event Planning and Catering is a Business

Event planning and catering is like any other business and for that business to run smoothly there must be rules. Those rules need to be written down in the form of a contract because some people don't believe in rules and without rules you have chaos.

Every event requires a contract, and it must be in writing, so simply stated; a contract is an agreement between two or more parties, creating legal mutual obligations for both parties.

Nearly all the events we did went smoothly but on a few occasions we had individuals who felt that rules did not apply to them and without rules that are enforceable you get chaos.

The Rule Breakers

The Republican Party West

One time we booked a function for the Republican Club West. It was going to be a simple function, just the facility, food, and media equipment for the speaker. Easy compared to the more lavish functions we normally book.

Anyway, we had booked the Claridge House on east 87th street and the food was to be standard sit-down menu: Appetizer, entrée and dessert, and a cash bar. If you are not familiar with a cash bar it operates like any other bar, guests can order whatever they want but are expected to pay and tip the bar staff after each round.

The function was booked two months prior to the actual function date, contracts signed by both parties and the initial fifty percent paid upon signing the contract.

The week of the Republican function I had lined up two other functions that week and we were in the process of assigning staff for each of the functions when I get a call form Earl, the Vice Chairman of the Republican Party West and he says he must cancel his function.

"Earl it is only two days before your function, the facility has been rented, food purchased and rental equipment on its way; not to mention that staff has already been assigned to your function." I told him.

"Yea I know" Earl says "but we must cancel so I need my deposit back" he says.

"I wish I could Earl, but it's two days before the function, money has be spent for your function and you are canceling just two days before the function date, there is no deposit to return." I told Earl.

Earl says to me "Listen this is the Republican Party you are talking to here. And we will sue you and your company if we don't get our despot back."

I tell Earl you signed a contract with the terms and conditions clearly stated and it says, and I quote:

"The client may cancel its function up to thirty calendar days prior to the Arrival Date without penalty. If a function is cancelled between seven through thirty calendar days prior to the function date, Client will be responsible for payment of 25% of the total catering fee. If the function is cancelled within seven calendar days or less of the function date, the client will be responsible for payment of 100% of the total catering fee."

"We are the Republican Party" Earl says again.

I tell Earl, "Listen, even if you were President Ronald Reagan there is no refund for you; have a nice day" and I hang up the phone. I guess Earl checked with a lawyer because I never heard from him again.

Liquor Licenses and Catering

I mentioned earlier that we were to have a cash bar at the Republican Party West function. As with all the catered events we did we supplied the usual sparkling water and soft drinks as well as wine and beer and sometimes hard alcohol.

In New York City if an active catering company is doing an event away from the main location you could get a "Temporary Beer, and Wine Permit, which authorizes the sale of wine, beer, or cider for consumption at a gathering for a period of 24 hours.

So, for any event off premises we would apply for a temporary liquor license at least two weeks prior to the event, In New York City you would apply to the State Liquor Authority or the SLA.

When Manhattan Parties provided hard alcohol (Vodka, Bourbon Rum and so forth) as with a cash bar, we applied for a temporary "Catering Permit", which is a one-day permit that authorizes an active on-premises retail licensee to provide all alcoholic beverages for use at a specific event located off the premises. Application must be received by the NY

State Liquor Authority at least two weeks prior to the event.

The Modeling Agency and the Event From Hell

Manhattan Parties catered several events for the "Ford Modeling Agency" as well as "Cover Girl Makeup "so we were familiar with working with models and had only the most pleasant of experiences with some of the models from these companies. Models like Christie Brinkley, Geri Carranza, and Lauren Hutton were always professional and pleasant.

In the 1980's many of the other models were not so pleasant and got terrible reputations for drug use, staying out all night at top disco clubs and being very rude and unprofessional.

Super model Gia Carangi for example was addicted to heroin and died of AIDS-related complication which she may have contracted from a contaminated heroin needle.

We were doing one of our monthly modelling events for one of the lesser-known modeling agencies, I don't remember which model was featured or the name of the modeling agency, but it was a small and supposedly up-and-coming agency.

During the 1980's there were several modeling agencies trying to be the next Ford Modeling Agency, and these lesser-known agencies basically took anyone who had the looks, male or female to become models.

However, many of these wannabe models did not possess the professionalism, demeanor, and quite frankly the class as a Christie Brinkley or a Geri Carranza.

Unfortunately for Manhattan Parties, we had booked "The Modeling Party From Hell' as the agency and the models they represented turned out to be less than professional and the function turned out to be a total nightmare.

We had rented 30 Lincoln Plaza which overlooked Central Park, I will describe this facility later in the book but for now it is suffice to say it has an Olympic size swimming pool, a sauna room, a large commercial restroom, and a full kitchen.

As with all events that Manhattan Parties did, we hired security to ensure the safety of the guests as well as our own safety.

For this event, security is stationed in the lobby of the building and in a specially designated elevator for the event guests. At the entrance to the function is additional security with two more security guards monitoring the actual function. Of course, our security guards are in plain clothes.

Within an hour of the function there are these no name models doing lines of cocaine in the restrooms. I am informed of this, and I go into the restroom to see this for myself and sure enough several models are doing lines of cocaine.

I ask the models to stop, telling them that it's illegal and the facility and my company could get in trouble.

One model says to me "Don't be a prude man! I mean who is going to know?" "Are you going to call the cops"

"Please" I say, No Coke at the function"

By now they are laughing and feeling good from the cocaine and one model says to me

"Listen Danny, do a line of cocaine, It will lighten you up" "Here you go, Do it"

She hands me a rolled up twenty-dollar bill and says to me

'Do a line or two, it will make will relax you are so tense"

I said, "no thanks, and if you do not stop I will have security throw all that cocaine down the toilet."

"Fuck you" Do you know who we are? Two models yell at me.

"Look, I don't care if you do cocaine, just don't do it here! "Go outside or something" I tell them.

In hindsight that was a big mistake on my part, because the twelve models took their cocaine and went outside to the back atrium of the building and did their lines of cocaine and came back to the party and then the party went all to hell.

Five of the aspiring models stripped naked, jumped into the pool and were swimming. The pool was for decoration, and we had no lifeguard on duty. If people wanted to swim we would have a lifeguard, but this was not a swimming party.

Another four of the so-called models were also naked having sex in the sauna room and the last three, well they were on the outside of rooftop pouring beer and wine onto the pedestrians on the sidewalk, laughing, and flashing their breasts.

Men and women were drunk, and more guests were dancing nude and making out. I looked around and things were out of hand. I mean it could have a been a scene from the swinger's club "Plato's Retreat", which was one of the first swinger's clubs that catered to heterosexual couples and bisexual men and women looking to hookup for sex. Of course, you could dance and enjoy a food buffet or just watch, but the club's main purpose was to hookup for sex.

I had to do something, and the rule of thumb is to cut the electricity and turn off the lights but for this function the way to go was to turn all the lights way up cut the music and have the cleaning crew come in and break the function down. It worked and within an hour everyone was out of the function.

The function only lasted three of the four hours it was contracted for, so I refunded the modeling agency the pro-rated amount for the one hour.

In my telephone conversation with this aspiring modeling agency, I informed them to lose Manhattan Parties telephone number and find another event planner for their next function and hung up.

Event Planning From Coffee to Caviar

Manhattan Parties provided catering for many of the "Maxwell House Coffee" television commercials that were shot in and around Manhattan. These commercials would start early in the morning usually around 7:00 am and end around 7:00 pm. So here we are providing breakfast and a late lunch scenario for a crew of about twenty-five.

Sunrise to Sunset

I recall one client, a Japanese filmmaker who wanted to shoot the sunrise over New 'York City's Central Park so Manhattan Parties rented the "Top

Of The One Club" which overlooked Central Park, and we provided bagels, cream cheese, and coffee from 4 am to 7 am for his crew of ten for two weeks straight until he got the exact shot he was looking for.

Music Videos

During the disco era we catered a few music videos for groups that are long forgotten. One hit wonders and groups that are disbanded. At the time we did event planning and catering for a few music videos for RCA records. The group "Odyssey" best known for their disco hit "Native New Yorker" I believe was one of the RCA recording artists.

For this shoot we supplied a few of the locations and the catering for a crew of about twenty-five, every night for a week. For the food it was mostly sandwiches and a few hot chafing dishes items.

Petrossian Caviar

Probably the most enjoyable function our company catered for was the monthly Petrossian Caviar tasting. Basically, our company provided the facility, equipment, ice and wait staff. Petrossian provided

Caviar and Stolichnaya Vodka. The monthly Petrossian Caviar tasting was a marketing tool for the Petrossian company whereby prospective clients would taste their product and enjoy good conversation and Russian vodka and in my opinion Petrossian Caviar is the best Caviar money can buy. Of course, I am a little biased because at the end of each tasting event I would get a tin of Petrossian Caviar as a thank you from Petrossian.

I would take my tin of the finest Caviar in the world home to my wife, and we would enjoy it with a bottle of Moët & Chandon champagne, and some extra crispy fried chicken.

Fried chicken you say, well the salty taste of caviar pairs great with the crunchy texture of the chicken and when you add a bottle or two of your favorite brut champagne it's heaven on your tongue.

The Bottom Line

Event planning can be very lucrative if you know what you are doing. The money is not in the food but in the services. Sure, food is important and profitable, but the real money is in the services. Let me explain, say you are event planning for a wedding, Manhattan parties would rent the facility and provide the food and service like most catering companies, but here is where we differ; Our company will also provide the music, the florist, the limousines and whatever else the client wants all for one price, no hidden extras.

Each one of these services pays Manhattan Parties a marketing fee of ten percent of their sale. Their cost of doing business, which is well worth it because of the repeat business we bring them.

Back in the early 1980 our average price per person was around $200.00 inclusive, which is around $750.00 per person today.

Business was excellent, and it was so hectic that I had to hire a limousine to take me from one event to the next.

Our rental facilities included mostly high-end residential locations like the Top Of The One Club in Lincoln Center, the Claridge House and 30 Lincoln Square. We also rented the Museum of Natural

History, parts of Central Park and even portions of Grand Central Station. From hot air balloons to yachts we rented almost anything a client wanted.

An example of one of the rental facilities we used a great deal was 30 Lincoln Square located on 62nd street and Central Park West. This was a rooftop facility totally enclosed in glass and overlooking Central Park. It had an outside rooftop deck that spanned 2.500 square feet, and the show piece of the facility was its dome covered Olympic size swimming pool.

The facility was complete with a full-size professional kitchen – NICE!

Typically for many of our events at this facility we would have a cold seafood buffet out by the pool area which would have whole cracked lobster and cracked Alaskan king crab, shrimp cocktail, oysters on the half shell and lots of Scottish smoked salmon. A large ice sculpture would be in the center of the seafood buffet and the pool would have a floral and light show display.

On the outside roof desk, were four hibachi stations where skewered quail, loins of pork and large prawns were roasted.

Inside, in addition to the standard hot buffet we had pasta, omelet, and carving stations of ribs of beef and wild roasted Turkey. A sushi station completed the food along with six standup bars positioned throughout the event.

For entertainment we had live music and either a magician or a caricature artist.

A must for each event is security, especially when you are doing a high-profile event like the television show "Entertainment Tonight" or a music Video. So, we would have security guards posted at the entrance of the facility and two security guards that would circulate in plain clothes throughout the event.

Lastly is the collection of payment for each event. The rule of thumb for high end catering is to take a deposit of fifty-cent of the fee upfront and then the balance before the event begins. That fifty percent deposit pays for the food, facility rental, entertainment and any special equipment needed.

The final payment covers the cost of our employees, and the balance is our profit, which is usually twenty-five percent of the selling price of the function.

Manhattan Parties would take a personal check or credit card or cash for the initial payment, but we always insisted on either a certified bank check or cash for the final payment. I mean you would be surprised how many famous and wealthy people will nickel and dime you.

They would say things like, "I thought you would have had more Shrimp Cocktail, or the band was not as good as I thought (the band the client chose) so I want twenty – percent off the final price.

If there is a legitimate concern, we would address it and refund monies if it was appropriate, by collecting the final payment before the event commences, puts Manhattan Parties in control not the client because you already have their money.

With relation to our staff, they were all independent contractors, so Manhattan Parties were not responsible for payroll taxes. Our only responsibility was to send to our staff and the IRS, Form 1099-NEC, which is an independent contractor form.

Some catering or event planners would pay their staff by check and at an hourly rate, and their staff might have to wait a week for their money.

Not at Manhattan Parties, you were paid in cash at the end of the function. Kitchen staff was paid $150.00 plus tips and wait staff were paid $100.00 plus tips. Managers were paid $200.00 plus tips.

Show Me The Money

I mentioned that high end catering and event planning is very lucrative, let me give you a financial rundown.

Using the dollar value of the 1980's let's say that you charge $200.00 per person, which includes not just the catering but everything I mentioned before. If your function has 100 guests then 100 X $200 = $20,000

For this event Manhattan Parties gets a marketing fee of 10 percent off the top: 10% X $20,000 = $2,000 marketing fee.

The profit margin for high end catering is twenty-five percent so in this scenario the profit would be $5,000

However, we also made an additional $2,000 in marketing fees so our profit on this one function is $7,000 which when you multiply by the number of functions per week (3) brings us to a weekly profit of $21,000 per week back in the 1980's, which today is equivalent to approximately $60,000. Not bad!

Of course, there are periods where you only get one function and some months where you do not have any functions. So, our average was approximately two functions per week and many times functions would have only 50 people so profit fluctuated.

Also, event planning is a 24 hour a day job, I mean for a Saturday night event my day would start at 7:00 am when food deliveries and catering rental equipment is delivered to the facility, and my day ends around midnight, when the facility is cleaned, and returned to its original state.

All Good Things Come to An End

After Jack left Manhattan Parties to pursue other ventures I decided not to continue with Manhattan

Parties for several reasons, but the main reason is that event planning is 7 days a week, 24 hours a day.

It is stressful enough with a partner but to handle operations alone would be too much. Also, I did not want to have to train a new partner because that would be double work.

So, I stopped taking functions and closed out the functions that we had which took almost 6 months to do. After that I decided to take a long-deserved rest.

You might have asked me why I did not have my wife or a relative in the business learning the ropes so when Jack left I would have had a replacement in the wings.

Well, my wife was now a Real Estate Broker and had opened her own business, Society Estates Inc, which was one of the premier real estate companies on the westside of Manhattan, so she had her hands full.

Let me tell you another of the basic rules of business which is to never go into business or hire family members or best friends to work for you.

Let me tell you the story of a friend who hired a family member to work in his restaurant. My friend hires his mother to work in his restaurant.

His mother works as the cashier of the restaurant. She learns quickly and is good at her job, maybe too good because she was stealing from the restaurant.

Apparently my friend noticed that the inventory and the sales did not match so he installed a video camera to watch the restaurant and low and behold he saw his own mother taking money out of the cash register drawer and putting the money in her purse.

Every night, five nights a week she helped herself to money in the cash drawer, so he had to question her, and he asked her why she was taking the money

Her response was something to the effect of well I could always use a few extra dollars and besides we are family.

The money is as much mine as it is yours. I am your mother! Unfortunately, he had to fire his mother for stealing. There you go!

Burger King Corporation

About a month after I had closed Manhattan Parties I got a call from a friend of mine, named Robert, he was with the Burger King Corporation, and they were going to try a new concept in Manhattan called Whopper Express.

It was to be a streamed lined version of Burger King's full-service menu. The new Whopper Express would offer the basics: Burgers, fish and chicken sandwiches, French fries, sodas, milkshakes and of course its signature item the" Whopper. "Also being an "Express" it has no seats like a traditional Burger King, just counters. The whole unit is approximately 1000 square feet from the front to the back of the kitchen.

I knew Manhattan like the back of my hand but more importantly I knew 42nd and 8th Avenue. I mean I spent a lot of time on 42nd street from my days working multi-unit operations with Nedick's corporation and my experience working the Biltmore, Roosevelt, and Milford Plaza hotels.

So, Robert sets me up in one of their Burger Kings in Manhattan and I train with a guy named Harry

Horowitz, who shows me the Burger King system, you know the basic stuff: Product development, paperwork, and computer systems. It takes four weeks of training and then I'm off to get these "Whopper Express" off the ground. Horowitz and I would go on to build a long-standing friendship that would last well over 20 years but more about that later in the book.

Whopper Express on 42nd. Street

Okay you may say to yourself I don't see any engineering or design experience in your portfolio Mr. Golio, so how do you build a Whopper Express with no such experience.

A Burger King franchise is like most other franchise operations, the corporate offices have already designed the unit, preordered the materials and equipment needed, subcontracted out the construction of the unit to an approved contractor and then they ship everything to the unit location. Very cookie cutter. Prefabricated like putting together a puzzle.

My job is to oversee the operation, to make sure the materials and equipment arrive and are put together according to the specifications set by the company.

Contractors are notorious for cutting corners and not getting the work done on time, someone must oversee the contractors and make sure that the work is finished on time and the unit opens as scheduled. That's part of my job.

Of course, positioning and putting together the equipment like the walk-in refrigerators and freezers is my job also. They are prefabricated just the way you assemble furniture you purchase at IKEA.

While construction is ongoing I am interviewing, hiring, and training staff for the restaurant. The rule of thumb in the restaurant industry is to hire 40 percent more staff than you need for the opening of a restaurant.

You see many people like the idea of working in a restaurant but very few people understand how hard restaurant work really is and the fast-food business is twice as hard as a full-service restaurant. I mean for one thing you are on your feet all day. Another is lunch. You get to eat at the end of your shift, which is usually between 2:30 pm - 3:00 pm when the restaurant's lunch rush ends.

Service needs to be quick; a customer should be able to place an order and get their food within 2 minutes so it's a high stress business. As a result, many employees go to lunch and never return and many employees just out and out quit, so you need to hire 40 percent more employees than you need until you can get a crew that is reliable.

After this unit is completed, units are then built on 23rd Street and 45th street, but it is the 42nd street unit that was my main base.

In the late 1980's Times Square was a dangerous place to be. Topless bars and peep shows were everywhere. I had a peep show directly across the street from the Whopper Express and down the block were adult theaters and countless sex shops.

Rolling Stone magazine had once declared West 42nd Street the "sleaziest block in America." In the evening and even during the day, 42nd street was an open meat rack of prostitution. Female and male prostitutes freely walked the street, and the sale of illegal drugs, robbery and murder was an everyday occurrence.

Times Square was also the headquarters for three-card monte players in the 1980s.

The three-card monte scam involves a dealer, a few shills and two lookouts who separate suckers from their money. Basically, shills (people who are part of the scam) win a few hands to induce unsuspecting people (usually tourists) to play. Usually, the dealer will let the tourist win a few hands to get them to think they can win the big money, and then the dealer manipulates the cards like a magician and the tourist loses. If the tourist wins and tries to pocket his winnings and walk away the tourist will get mugged by one of the lookouts around the corner. Only the three card monte players win.

 One day a group of three card monte players set up shop in front of Whopper Express. I see this and go out and tell them to leave or I will call the police. They leave but come back the next day. It was a losing proposition; business was down because of the environment.

I mean people were afraid to come into the restaurant. I needed to do something. So, one day I told one of the three card monte players to come into my office and I told him "Listen, I know you must make a living, but you can't stay in front of my store. If I must call the police every day I will, which I know will screw up your business and maybe get you arrested." So, then I said "Look, I spoke to the manager of Tad's Steak, and you can stay on the side between Whopper Express and Tads Steak, but you need to spend some money in Whopper Express and in Tad's.

"What" Are you shaking me down" he says with a smile.

"Not at all, think of it as the cost of doing business, so 10 percent of the take would work. Come on give me a break, It's a good deal and we will both make out what do you say? "I told him.

On any given day, a monte crew can earn $1,500 or more, and with more than twelve three card monte teams operating on 42nd. Street at that time, competition can be tough. So, he says yea no problem and every day the monte crew buys $75.00

worth of French Fries from both restaurants, which increase sales and because French fries are low cost and high profit the sales reduces our overall food cost percentage.

Years later over a dinner at the "Cattleman", a steakhouse located on east 45th street in Manhattan, my friend Robert who was now the Regional Vice President of the company asked me how I kept my food and labor costs so low, so I told him the story of three card monte and as he laughs he says

"I knew it wasn't your great skills in food cost and labor control"

The Cattleman by the way was the restaurant used for the photoshoot of the 1966 remake of the John Wayne classic "Stagecoach" which starred among others my fellow member and President of the "William Holden Wildlife Foundation," the award-winning actress Stefanie Powers from the long running television series "Hart To Hart."

Anyway, 42nd street back then was a tough place to work and there were characters of all sorts roaming the streets. It was tough keeping them out of Whopper Express.

One day a thug comes into Whopper Express and starts putting shirts he most likely stole from the nearby Bonds men clothing store on the counter and tries to sell the shirts to my customers. I tell this guy to get out, but he just ignores me. We got into a heated argument and then the thug pulled out a knife, so I backed away.

Lucky for me the beat cop, Tom sees this, and enters the restaurant. He puts his two fingers up to his lips to give me the shush sign and sneaks up behind the thug and put his 45-caliber pistol to the thug's head and presses the barrel into his temple.

"Hey, how's it going Dan", Tom says to me, the barrel of his gun still pressed hard into the thug's temple.

"Great Tom, now that you are here" I say

This guy freezes, drops the knife and Tom handcuffs him. Everyone in the restaurant, the customers and employees start to applaud; Tom takes a bow as he drags him out of the restaurant.

It was like that back then in Manhattan, there were beat cops walking the streets and for me Tom always stopped in once a day to see how things were going.

With police the rule of thumb is 'Police Eat Free" Why? Because when you call them they will come and come fast. I mean your restaurant becomes sort of their restaurant and you can count on the police to be there in a heartbeat.

Years later I was riding the #2 train in Manhattan and this freaky guy came up to me and said hello to me.

His hair is all cut up in sections and it is blue, and his body is covered with tattoos.

I look at him and ask him" Do I know you."

He says to me "Dan, it's me Tom, Tom O'Hara, the cop,

We hug and shake hands and I say "Tom, what are you doing on this train looking like that"

Tom tells me he is part of the New York City Narcotics Division and the New York Drug Enforcement Task Force.

"Really Tom" I say

"Yea, my unit is attached to the Investigators Unit working with the Assistant District Attorney."

The train stops at 42nd. street and Tom says to me "Well this is my stop and gives me his card"

"Call me and let's catch up" he says, as he exits the train.

"Will do" I say as Tom disappears into the train station.

This was the 42nd. Street in the mid-1980s. It was filled with dangerous, sleezy and sometimes colorful characters like the naked cowboy, who would roam the streets of 42nd street naked, except for the guitar he had strung over his shoulder and sing to the tourists or the religious fanatics with signs that said the "The World Is Coming To An End -Repent."

I had completed the three Whopper Expresses for the Burger King corporation, all were running well, and I told corporate that I was thinking of moving on, but they convinced me to stay with promises of new Whopper Expresses to open and new ideas that were coming out of corporate. And of course, the great persuader – Money! So, just when I thought I was out they dragged me back in.

Free Delivery And The BOGO Coupon

The Burger King corporation was the first fast food franchise to offer free delivery and since Whopper Express was part of the Burger King corporation we offered free delivery as well. So, I hired a crew of 15 delivery guys, 5 for each of the three Whopper expresses and we were off.

Delivery was a good idea, the Whopper Express units on 23rd street and 45th street did very well. Office building would call in orders and sales skyrocketed. It was not unheard of to get lunch orders of fifty to seventy-five Whoppers per order. Business was booming even at the 42nd street location.

But at the 42nd. Street location we had only a few offices, but we had a plethora of the – SEEDY!

I mean our clientele were tourists and the seedy side of society; topless bars, peep shows, porn shops and lots of pimps with girls working the street. At Whopper express we did not discriminate, and money is money, so we delivered to all of them.

I mean pimps would place orders for themselves and their stable of prostitutes, the topless bars would order for the dancers and my delivery guys were busy round the clock.

After a while I became sort of a local celebrity, I was the guy with the whoppers, the guy who delivers, Burgers, fries, and fish sandwiches to the working girl; I mean pimps and topless dancers knew me, the porn shop owners would come in and kibbitz with me. My friend Sam, who managed Tad's Steakhouse next to the Whopper Express would laugh and tell me that I was the Burger Pimp of 42nd. street.

For those of you who do not know, Tad's Steak House was a very low-end steak house using cheap cuts of meat whereby a customer could get a 14-ounce rib eye steak, a baked potato, salad, and bread all for the unbelievable price of $9.99.

Anyway, we delivered to anyone, even my future mother-in-law. Her name was Connie and like clockwork three times a week; every Monday, Wednesday and Thursday, my future mother-in-law would place her delivery order which consisted of three orders each of Whoppers, chicken and fish sandwiches and fries for a total of twelve items.

Connie, my future mother-in-law lived at Pearl Street, which is in the financial district of New York City, so it was a twenty-minute plus ride for the delivery guy or a one-hour ride in both directions.

Of course, Connie wanted the delivery made during the height of the lunch rush, so my delivery guy was out of action and of course since she was my future mother-in-law there was no charge.

Whopper Express was also one of the first fast food operations to offer BOGO coupons (Buy one, get one). Basically, a customer goes into the restaurant with a coupon and gets either 2 whoppers, or 2 chicken or 2 fish sandwiches for the regular price of a whopper. However, they must purchase either a soda or a fry to get this deal.

The whopper in this case is what's called a "loss leader" or an item that is purposefully sold at a loss or for less than market value to attract new customers or gain additional revenue on the sale of other items such as soda or fries.

For us the BOGO was also a way of tracking where our customers were coming from. So, they were color coded, different colors for different blocks. For example, a Yellow coupon might be used for the 42nd. and Broadway area and a blue coupon for 42nd. and 8th Avenue. Then counting where most of the colors are coming from gives you an idea where the bulk of your business comes from.

Like I mentioned there were many characters roaming the streets of 42nd street in the mid-1980s and sometimes you can be surprised by whom you meet. I remember once this unbelievably attractive woman comes into Whopper Express and orders a whopper with cheese no pickles. As she ate her whopper I said to myself; this is the most attractive women I have ever seen except for my wife of course. Later I found out that she was Vanessa Williams, former Miss America, actress and singer.

Or the time this guy comes into Whopper Express he is all hyped up and he has a stretch limousine waiting outside the restaurant with four people in it.

He says to me that he would like to purchase five of my Burger King hats. At that time our employee hats had a BK in the front.

I told him I can't sell employee uniforms to customers. He says, "I'm Ben Kingsley." Your hats have a BK in front" and he points to the Burger King initials on our employee hats "See BK for Ben Kingsley."

I had absolutely no idea who this guy was, let alone who Ben Kingsley was. So, I told him "Listen I wish I could sell you the hats, but they are reserved for my employees, and I'm not allowed to sell employee uniforms to customers I am sorry."

I can see that he is frustrated especially since he realized that I had no idea who he was, so he just left.

Later I found out he was Ben Kingsley; the actor who won the academy award for his portrayal of Gandhi.

But then there are the oddities that lead to strange liaisons. There was a guy named Benny, he was an older, short man who always wore a black tuxedo. He had a cane, only it wasn't a cane, I mean it was a magic stick, and he would make flowers come out of it; Benny was an actual magician.

Benny would come into the Whopper express twice a week and order a Jr. whopper and fries and he would pay for his meal and leave.

Joe Franklin

One day Benny the Magician comes into the Whopper Express and starts to talk to me and tells me that he will be on the "Joe Franklin Show and to watch him on WOR channel 9 in Manhattan.

For those of you who do not know Joe Franklin, he was a radio and television host personality who was on WOR from 1962 until 1993,

Franklin's guests included an eclectic mix of actual celebrities and low-level performers. People like Benny the magician or the tap-dancing dentist or the singing frankfurter cart guy from the corner of 40th and 6th Avenue and this eclectic mix of odd performers would be on the same panel with celebrities such as Woody Allen, Bette Midler, Howard Stern, Al Pacino, Barbara Streisand, Michael Jackson, and Joe Franklin's long-time childhood friend actor Tony Curtis.

Anyway, the next day, Benny wanted me to meet Joe Franklin, so I went up to Joe Franklin's office on West 42nd. street and met him, and he is very cordial, and we talk for a while and Benny tells him that I have the Whopper Express up the block, Joe mentions that he loves hamburgers so the next day I send him a few Whoppers and within a week we sort of developed a friendship.

I would go up to his cluttered office at least twice a week. I met Tiny Tim "Tiptoe Through the Tulips" at Joe's office. His real name was Herbert Buckingham Khaury, a genuine nice guy, Tiny Tim became an acquaintance of mine along with Joe Franklin.

Mr. Franklin was a gentle man with an unbelievable amount of knowledge of movies past and present. It became sort of a routine, Benny the magician would come to the Whopper Express and I would give him a bag of Whoppers and fries which he would take to Joe Franklin. Every once in a while Joe would give the Whopper Express a plug on the air telling his viewers something to the effect like: "Today I had lunch with my friend Dan at the Whopper Express on 42nd and 6th Avenue, it's a great place for burgers."

Is It Real Or Did You Make It Yourself

Back then and especially on 42nd. street it was not unusual to get counterfeit money.

Counterfeit money is currency produced illegally in a deliberate attempt to imitate that currency and deceive its recipient.

Money made by the United States has a specific type of feel to it and people who handle money often, such as managers and cashiers, can identify lower-quality counterfeit money just by touching it. You see, the United States uses a specific non-commercial paper for its money and the printed ink is slightly raised. Also, each bill denomination has a different weight so if you handle money often you should be able to spot a counterfeit bill. I should also say here that the most counterfeited bills are the $20.00 and $50.00 bill because they will give you the biggest bang for your buck so to speak.

So, if a counterfeiter passes a $20.00 bill they try to order something that costs one or two dollars so they can get back eighteen dollars (real money).

With all that said, you must keep in mind I am working on the "sleaziest block in America" according to Rolling Stone magazine and the people on this street can be inventive.

People who pass counterfeit money in fast food places and restaurants are not the counterfeit geniuses you see in movies or television, but rather ordinary people using low-key methods and the counterfeiters on West 42nd street are basically junkies, prostitutes, and the low criminal element, who roam the streets of 42nd. street. So high tech counterfeiting is pretty much out of the question.

Once I caught a guy passing phony five-dollar bills, he must have been high because he was passing photocopies of five-dollar bills, and in black and white no less.

There was this other time when a customer handed me a fifty-dollar bill at the 45th street location, I looked at the bill and it looked good and had the right feel but for some reason the bill bothered me, so I took a special "Marker Pen" that detects genuine US currency paper and used it on the bill. Basically, all you need to do is draw a mark on the bill: dark mark means fake; light mark passes test.

The fifty-dollar bill passed the test, but I don't know what it was, but the bill still bothered me.

Suddenly it hit me, this guy separated a fifty-dollar bill into two parts and then pasted the front of the fifty-dollar bill, onto to the front of a one-dollar bill.

The bill passed the counterfeit marker test because it was real US currency paper.

So, I look at him and crumble the fake bill in front of him and toss it in the garbage can and I say to him,

"Listen you got any real money" He smiles and walks away.

Apparently the front and back of US currency is printed on separate runs and then put together so if you know how, and work at it long enough you can separate the front and the back into two pieces.

Keep in mind that the purpose of passing counterfeit money is to get as much real money as possible and counterfeiters and quick-change artists prey on busy operations, like bars and fast-food operations when these establishments are at their busiest in hopes of slipping the phony bills past the bartender, cashier, or manager.

As such, there are rules for proper cash handling; for example, the rule of making sure all the bills that go into a cash drawer are face up is a double check to ensure that the dollar bills have the proper presidential portraits on them.

As you read this let me ask you this?

Do you know which president is on a ten, twenty or fifty-dollar bill? And what about the back of each of these bills; which building is on the back of these bills? Yea, I know you don't know.

The criminals who counterfeit know the answer and they are gambling that the average person has no idea about the money that have in their pocket.

You should also keep in mind that if an establishment gets stuck with a counterfeit bill, there is no reimbursement for it and the establishment is out of luck.

The counterfeit bill needs to be reported to the government and if you pass the counterfeit bill to someone else as change you could be considered a criminal – SUCKS RIGHT!

Okay so how do you spot counterfeit money?

There are several ways to spot counterfeit money. Here are six of the most obvious ways to spot phony money.

- Use a maker pen to see if the paper is genuine US Currency – Dark mark means fake; light mark passes test.
- Counterfeit money will Lack quality printing and look dull without fine detail
- The presidential portrait will be dull or smudgy
- Have the correct portrait for the currency denominations. (I once got a twenty-dollar bill that had a portrait of Michael Jackson in the front and not Andrew Jackson – go figure.)
- Legal paper has small blue and red treads that run thru the paper
- Make sure that the serial numbers on a bill match, and are evenly spaced
- Newer bill have a metallic strip that runs thru the bills

It was like the wild west on West 42nd. street in those days and it would not be until the 1990's that Mayor Guliani would clean up Time square, but until that time it was becoming increasingly dangerous. I mean we were robbed at both our 45th street and 42nd street location at gun point a few times.

The last time we were robbed I was standing behind the cashier bagging the food order. Bagging means that as the order is called out I assemble the order say a Whopper, fries and a soda and put it in a Whopper Express bag while the cashier rings up the sale.

This time when the cashier asked the customer how he was going to pay, cash, coupon, or both, he responded that he would be paying with GUN and pulled out a 38-caliber pistol and fired two shots in the air. He grabs the money and runs out of the restaurant. Luckily no one was injured.

After a while it got so bad that someone stole two large silver bullet garbage cans with the garbage still in them, at the height of business.

With the streets of 42nd street getting worse I decided it was time to move on. The hotel industry was in a slump in New York City, and I really did not want to start up my catering business, but as luck would have it I got a call from a Headhunter in the food service industry. A Headhunter by the way is a person who identifies and approaches suitable candidates employed elsewhere and steals them away to work for the company they represent.

He says he got my name from a guy he knew named Larry who said he worked with me at JFK International Airport and that I had a lot of multi-unit experience.

The headhunter goes on to say that he knows about Nedick's multi-unit experience and that I currently helped build the three Whopper Expresses I am managing now. So, I'm perfect!

Larry goes on to say that this is the position of a lifetime, and I can write my own ticket, money is no object.

I say okay l will take the interview, and with that, I land the position of developing the largest "Dunkin Donut Kitchen In The World"

Dunkin Donuts of America

After my time as District Manager at Burger King, I landed a job with the Riese Organization in New York City. The Riese Organization was started by Murray and Irving Riese in 1936 and went on to become the nation's largest privately owned restaurant entity operating over 150 restaurants.

At one time or another the company owned restaurants such as: Childs, Longchamps, Luchows, Schrafft's, Beefsteak Charlie's, Chock Full O'Nuts, Pizza Hut and KFC to name a few.

I was hired as an opener and manager for the company. My job was to oversee the building, organization, training and running of what was to become the largest Dunkin Donuts of America kitchen in the world. That's right – THE WORLD!

Murry and Irving Riese had cut a deal with the Dunkin Donuts corporation to open 20 Dunkin franchised stores in the New York Metro area. There would be one flagship store and 19 satellite units.

A satellite unit means that it was a Dunkin Donut but with the baking done off premise in a centralized kitchen and shipped twice a day to each of the 19 satellite units.

If you want to own a Dunkin Donuts franchise, you need to graduate from Dunkin Donuts University. Yes you read that right. Dunkin Donuts had their own university. As a franchisee if you fail the courses, you do not get a franchise. At that time the fee for the university was $10,000 per franchisee.

Murray and Irving Riese were too old and too busy with over 150 restaurants to attend Dunkin Donuts University, so they put a team together of their best employees: The team consisted of their best Regional District Manager, their best company baker and me.

With the team picked, we were off to Dunkin Donuts University in Braintree, Massachusetts.

Dunkin Donuts University

Located in Braintree, Massachusetts, a small town with a population of under 33,000 people, it was more rural than urban. Braintree was a peaceful community, the motel and almost all the restaurants closed at 9:00 pm. So, you could imagine the frustration of guys who came from the city the never sleeps "New York City" looking for something to do after dark.

The big draw in Braintree was the local Friendly's Restaurant that stayed open until 11:00 pm.

We were there for the eight-week training course which consisted of Dunkin Donuts management systems and of course baking.

To graduate from the University, you had to cut, fry and finish all by hand 140 dozen saleable donuts in 6 hours, if you failed and still wanted a franchise it's another $10,000 to repeat the course. You see in those days Dunkin Donuts had integrity and wanted to make sure you made a good product and that as a franchisee you succeeded. Why? because Dunkin Donuts got a six percent royalty and a four percent, marketing fee off the top every month for the life of the franchise.

So, every day from Monday to Friday we would travel to the University to make the donuts and on the weekends I would fly home to Manhattan on People Express.

In 1981, People Express was one of the first low-cost USA airlines. All seats were the same price except for slightly lower "off-peak" fares. Fares were paid in cash aboard the aircraft early in the flight. I guess people back then were more honest. I mean I paid with a personal check which I wrote while riding on the plane. In the 1980's, computer access was limited regarding banking so if someone wrote a check and it bounces, People Express may not find out for a week or two. A little late since the flight came and gone and by 1987 so did People Express.

The company had rented motel rooms for all three of us in Braintree, Massachusetts but Braintree was sort of a hick town, so we went back to New York on the weekends.

The Riese Organization paid for my travel as part of my employment contract, but it was tiring traveling back and forth on the weekend to New York City. So, I asked the company to forgo my plane fare and put me up at the Boston Park Plaza Hotel in central Boston instead.

I mean if you calculate the cost of airfare or even train fare and a cab to and from the airport or train station it was more expensive to travel than to put me up at the hotel, so the company agreed.

Every morning from Monday to Friday I would emerge in my khaki-colored Dunkin Donuts uniform and get into a black town car and head to the University, and then return covered in bread flour and head to my room at the hotel.

I was able to fly my fiancé out to 'Boston a few times to stay with me at the hotel and that made the job more palatable.

The hotel had a fabulous brunch every Saturday and Sunday. At that time, it was only $35.00 per person for the best brunch I ever had.

In the hotel's white tablecloth dining room, waiters poured unlimited Moet e Chandon champagne as the pianist played the latest tunes on a Steinway piano and several food stations surrounded the dining tables.

 For breakfast there was an omelet station where omelets are made to order along with Belgian waffles, bacon, and sausage.

A seafood station consisted of Smoked Salmon, cold shrimps and lobster tails and cracked Alaskan Crab legs and three carving stations of Turkey, Ham and Ribs of Beef completed the food stations.

For dessert the hotel brought out its Venetian table which had a dazzling array of pastries, cakes, frozen desserts, fresh fruit, and coffees.

After the weekend it's back to work and time to make the donuts. It was hard work and draining but we tried hard to do well and give the Riese organization their monies worth.

After the laborious work of making donuts all day, the Regional District Manager (RDM) and I usually shoot some hoops to unwind.

 On the evening before the final donut cutting test, we are shooting hoops and the RDM says to me "Dan I think I just sprained my wrist"

"Really I said" Are you sure? We must cut donuts tomorrow"

"Yea" he said, "I'm not going to be able to cut donuts tomorrow, my wrist hurts really bad." It's up to you and Bobby." He told me. Bobby was the head baker

So, it's 6:00 am and the two remaining employees of the Riese organization take the donut test. One of us must pass for the Riese organization to get the franchise for twenty Dunkin Donut franchises.

There are several potential franchisee owners also taking the test along with us, all of which must pass this test of mixing, rolling, cutting, frying, and finishing 140 dozen saleable donuts in 6 hours to get a franchise.

Cutting the donuts is a problem because the donut bench, the table where you roll and cut the dough is long and high. I am not that tall, so I stand on a chair and literally jump onto the donut bench and begin rolling and cutting donuts; cake donuts first and then yeast donuts.

This is a process because once the dough is rolled out, you must cut the donuts using the correct donut cutter and then toss the donut to the other hand to give the donut a stretch with your index and forefinger and then place the donut onto a frying screen all in one motion.

Once the donuts are cut, I then fry them in a large frying vat turning them with drumsticks. When the donuts are fried the rack is pulled out of the oil and placed on a draining rack. This process is done several times until all the donuts are fried.

I managed to cut the required 140 dozen saleable donuts in 2 -1/2 hours. Next comes finishing by either filling donuts with crème or jelly and then finishing the tops with icings or dipping the donuts in chocolate. I completed the test in only four hours.

The master baker for the Riese Organization, Bobby is struggling. It's one thing to bake bread or specially desserts but cutting donuts is hard work. It takes speed, accuracy, and stamina to cut, fry and finish 140 salable donuts and I think he was out of shape for this test, so he failed.

The Regional District Manager was delighted that I passed and immediately called the Riese organization and told him we got the franchise. Amazedly within hours of me passing the test his wrist got better – Go figure!

Building the Donut Franchise

Back in New York, our head baker went back to the Riese organization baking breads and cookies and the Regional District Manager (RDM) went back to his duties overseeing more than 50 Riese food establishments within Penn and Grand Central Station.

We started building the largest Donut Kitchen in the world. The Reise Organization has picked Penn Station as the location for the kitchen. This location was picked because the idea was that we would build satellite units throughout Penn station and Grand Central station and in midtown from 42nd. street and 2nd avenue to 50th street and Broadway.

Penn station was a perfect transportation hub for this. It took a few months to layout the kitchen and equipment and set up a product and shipping schedule. We built the flagship Dunkin Donuts within feet from the central kitchen.

When that's done we hired and trained the staff. Most of whom came from other restaurant franchises that the Reise organization owned.

When you open a Dunkin Donut franchise you must use Dunkin Donut approved computer registers. Each register as an opening balance number that must be sent to Dunkin Donuts main headquarters. At the close of each day register readings are taken, a beginning balance and an ending balance; then a cash report is filled out and the register tape is attached to the report.

Dunkin Donuts

This tells Dunkin Donuts what the sales were for that day. It is from these reports that Dunkin Donuts calculates its six percent commission and four percent marketing fee.

Finding bakers and good employees was hard and I interviewed literally hundreds of potential employees to find a crew of 20 to work in the central kitchen. Bakers, however, was another story, The one or two bakers I hired did not last long and I found myself working seven days a week cutting donuts at night and managing the unit during the day.

Even though I lived in Manhattan the work was so grueling I asked the Riese organization to put me up at the Penta Hotel across the street from Penn station.

I had a room at the Penta hotel for over one year. My wife was in London at the time, so being at the hotel was not so bad.

Jimmy the Greek

Once I got out of the kitchen and began my management duties, I began to go to different coffee shops in Manhattan in search of qualified donut bakers. I literally traveled all over Manhattan, the Bronx and Brooklyn with little or no luck at all because most of the coffee shops or restaurants purchased prepackaged donuts.

It was not until I found myself on 14th street and 7th Avenue and went into a small coffee shop that sold donuts. I ordered a coffee and a glazed donut.

To my surprise and delight the donut was excellent. I asked the guy at the counter who made this glazed donut.

"Hey buddy" I said, "Who made this donut?"

The guy at the counter says to me "Why you don't like it?"

So, I told him it was a good donut and that I have been trying to get a donut as good as this for a few weeks.

Then I said to him" Do you own this place?"

"No" "Why do you want to know?" he said

Then I went on to tell him that I was with Dunkin Donuts and that I am looking for a head donut baker and that I would like to hire him.

After some bartering back and forth he agreed, and I got myself a real master donut baker.

Jimmy was old school Greek, he was in his fifties, thin and could cut over 100 dozen donuts in no time. He smoked Kent cigarettes while he worked, all business and was always on time.

By now I had gotten two baker trainees to learn the donut business and had a crew of 20 employees mixing, and finishing the donuts, muffins, and croissants. The croissants were the easy part because the croissants came frozen in a box, all you had to do was give them a little twist like a horseshoe, put them in the proof box and then bake for 15 minutes easy as pie.

With the baking under control, I now was able to manage the flagship restaurant and set up the 19 satellite donut units.

A little-known fact about these satellite units is that the average customer never knew that there was no baking done on the premises. Why? Because each satellite unit had a special air flow system that pumped artificial donut aroma through the unit so customers would smell the donuts being made but it was just smoke and mirrors as the aroma came from chemicals not actual baking of the donuts.

The integrity of Dunkin Donuts at the time was quality and freshness. For example, yeast donuts have a shelf life of 12 hours and cake donuts a shelf life of eight hours after which they are to be discarded, however the Reise organization could not understand why perfectly good donuts should be discarded, so they started bringing the donuts to be discarded to their "Martin's Coffee Shops" and sold the donuts under the Martin's name.

Selling the Dunkin Donuts brand under a different name was against the franchise agreement and against Dunkin Donut policy. If a franchisee committed such a violation, Dunkin Donuts would pull the franchise, however, this is the Riese organization, one of the largest privately held restaurant corporations in the United States that had built the largest Dunkin Donut kitchen in the world with a commitment to build twenty Dunkin Donuts units in New York City, so this matter had to be handled in a diplomatic way to say the least.

Dunkin Donuts demanded that Riese organization have one of their own District managers monitor this situation to ensure the integrity of their Donuts or they will pull all twenty franchises.

With that demand, it was mutually agreed that I would be the Dunkin Donuts District manager.

I was then employed by both the Riese organization and Dunkin Donuts to do just that.

So, part of my duties was to ensure that donut shelf life holding times were met and that donuts that passed the shelf life were discarded.

At one point the Dunkin Donuts corporate office offered me a franchise of my own. It was a great deal; Dunkin Donuts would loan me the money without interest to build the store and as an owner I would pay the usual royalty and marketing fees to Dunkin Donuts plus an additional set amount to repay the loan.

At that time, the average Dunkin Donut owner netted about $75,000 per year. I knew this was a high stress business, I mean the average Dunkin Donut owner lasted approximately five years before he got burned out and would sell his store. At the time Dunkin Donuts had a policy that if you could not sell your store they would buy it back at cost.

I declined the offer because the amount of work the donut business was in relation to the amount of money I would make was not for me.

In the two years I had been a district manager for Dunkin Donuts I was already burned out and ready to leave the company.

Years later when I was teaching at the New York Restaurant School, Dunkin Donuts had contacted me because they were in disarray and needed help in getting Dunkin Donuts back on track.

I left this job because it was the job from hell and the amount of work needed to put Dunkin Donuts back on track would have been enormous, so I declined.

Two weeks later, Dunkin Donuts called again and tried to lure me back asking me what it would take to bring me back. I told them I would want $250,000.00 thinking that the dollar amount was way over what they were willing to pay, however a week later they called back and agreed to my offer. I declined.

Like Father Like Son

While the Dunkin Donuts commercial slogan was "Time To Make The Donuts", mine had become "Time Not To Make the Donuts."

I had decided to go into teaching like my dad. He taught mechanical drawing and drafting at Stuyvesant High School in Manhattan, so I guess I followed in my father's footsteps.

At this time money was not a concern for me because I had made a great deal of money from my Manhattan Party Company and Dunkin Donuts had paid me very well in salary, bonus money and perks.

I knew teaching was not going to pay me the same as being in the business, but it was a way to start to work less and enjoy life more, and to give back, and impart some of the knowledge I learned over the years to others.

After consulting with my dad, I made the decision to apply for a vocational teaching license in Cafeteria and Catering from the New York City Board of Education.

My education and experience qualified me for a vocational teaching license, however I still needed to take some college courses in teaching methodology which I got online at the University of Missouri. Once completed I applied for my vocational teaching license.

Acquiring a vocational teaching license was a three-part process:

First there was a written test which I easily passed. Second was the interview process which went well and lastly was a practical test.

A practical test is a performance test in a kitchen to see if you can cook. It is sort of like a Food Network television show where chefs are asked to create a five-course meal from scratch with ingredients found in the kitchen; all of which had to be completed in one hour.

The difference is that we were all potential vocational teachers not celebrity chefs.

Grading is based on taste, presentation and whether you can complete the five courses in the time allotted.

As luck would have it, the practical test was administered by my culinary professor from New York Technical College, professor Veal.

After quick survey of the ingredients, I quicky decide on a Caprice Salad for the appetizer, Penne ala Aglio e Olio for the second, Shrimp Scampi and grilled Lamb chops for the third and fourth and a simple strawberry and whipped cream for dessert.

The key to success here is timing as to what to do first. It is timing where a real chef excels, and amateurs fail.

All the menu items that I have picked I have made hundreds of times before when I was a Sous Chef and all the items take fifteen minutes or less to cook, so completing the test in one hour is a piece of cake, no pun intended.

Some of the potential teachers tried to do too much, for example making chicken soup from scratch, I mean it takes over an hour just to cook the chicken properly.

One potential teacher thought he was going to show his great culinary expertise by making potato gnocchi in a marinara sauce from scratch. While it takes only a few minutes or so to cook the gnocchi, you must boil, cool, peel and mash the potatoes; this process alone takes approximately thirty-five to forty minutes. To complete the recipe including the sauce takes at least one hour. If you were able to complete the gnocchi in time you still had four more items to complete.

Timing is the key to success in a working kitchen and the sign of a real chef. These guys most likely never worked in a working kitchen because they had no sense of timing, and most failed the test.

Within a short period of time, I am a licensed vocational teacher looking for a school to teach in. I land a temporary position teaching cooking 101 at Park West Public High School located in what was called "Hell's Kitchen." Later Park West High School was renamed "Food and Finance High School."

By the way the name "Hell's kitchen" was coined by the famous frontiersman, congressman, and legendary hero of the Alamo Davy Crockett who on a visit to New York City in 1835 said the following:

"'In my part of the country, when you meet an Irishman, you find a first-rate gentleman; but these are worse than savages; they are too mean to swab hell's kitchen."

The area that Davy Crockett was referring to was "Five Points" which was located on Manhattan's upper east side where mostly Irish and Italians settled in the early 1800's.

Later however, the Irish moved to Hell's Kitchen, which was the area from 41st to 59th Street on the west side of Manhattan. It was a high crime area with Irish gangs like the Gopher Gang led by One Lung Curran and later by Owney Madden. Later it was the home base of the Irish mob the "Westies" who were aligned with the Gambino crime family. Hell's kitchen became known as the most dangerous area on the American Continent.

Upper Manhattan especially Pleasant Avenue and Mulberry street in lower Manhattan was primarily Italian and the home of the Italian Mafia.

Anyway, Park West High School was smack in the middle of Hell's Kitchen, and it was not unusual for me to have students put their knives, guns, and machetes in my desk drawer until class was over. Back then Park West High school was not a great place to work. This is the time before metal detectors or security guards.

The New York Restaurant School (NYRS)

I see an ad in the New York times for a restaurant management teaching position at the New York Restaurant school.

So, I interviewed for the teaching position at the New York Restaurant School (NYRS) on 34th street and 6th Avenue in Manhattan and low and behold the interviewer is my friend from my fast-food days Harry Horowitz. We get to talking and Harry goes on to say that the program is new, and the owner of the school has high hopes for this management program. As far as he is concerned I got the job, but I still need to meet with the Director of Education, and he is the final word.

The following week I met with the Director of Education, and he offered me the position and I accepted, and he takes me to Harry's office and tells Harry that I am hired and to get me acclimated with the program.

As we talk I ask Harry where the lesson plans for the management course are, Harry takes out a large three ring binder and says "Well, we don't really have any lesson plans just these articles from magazines and newspapers to use in your lecture."

While I am looking dumfounded, he says and "Dan, this Friday is going to be my last day because I am staring a new company called 'Potato Country'."

"You mean I have to start this program on my own" I say. "

"I know you and I know you will not have any problems succeeding, besides if you have any problems or just want to talk here is my office address." Harry told me.

World Of Work

NYRS was to develop a new type of management program in which the students would be pre-hired before they graduate the program was called "World of Work, "but the fly in the ointment is that the program had no agreements signed with restaurant companies to pre-hire students, nor was there any actual lesson plans written for this program.

Moreover, management classes were to be held at

the New School For Social Research, a graduate-level university founded in 1919 located at 6 E 16th St, New York, NY 10003 and not NYRS.

Harry helped with setting up a few restaurant companies, and using my contacts with Restaurant Associates, the Riese Organization, Burger King, McDonald's, and Dunkin Donuts I was able to get pre-hire agreements signed so there was enough assignments to go forward.

As friends and associated I would often meet and talk with Harry about the NYRS management program and "Potato Country."

Let me digress a little here and explain what "Potato Country" was. It was a group of vending carts positioned on the streets of New York City that would sell freshly cut French fried potatoes.

Sounds good but this is New York City and in Harry's zeal in going into this market he forgot two important rules of Manhattan, which Harry taught me by the way, which was first location, location, and location. The areas where the Potato Country carts were located were not prime locations and had little foot traffic.

Prime locations were taken up the frankfurter carts which for the most part were controlled by organized crime.

Second, people in Manhattan want things fast like they want it yesterday and to wait until potatoes are cut and fried takes too long in the "Big Apple."

The NYRS Management Program had taken off and soon we had more classes than I could handle so I asked Harry if he wanted to come back to teaching. He said yes and abandoned the fledging potato vending cart business.

Let me just say that I have worked with a lot of managers in my many years in the restaurant business and Harry Horowitz is the best restaurant manager in the business bar none. I have often said that if I opened a restaurant I would only hire the best to manage my restaurant and the best is Harry Horowitz.

Okay enough about my friend and associate. With Harry's help the program expanded into a 2-year degree program and combined with the NYRS Culinary Arts programs was very successful for many years.

Students were pre-hired, graduated and went to work for some of the best well-known establishments of that time. The general manager of" Tavern On The Green" was one of my students. Top management positions held by NYRS graduate students included: "Russian Tea Room, Windows On The World" and "Burger King" to name a few.

Of course, with all successes there are the occasional failures, for example, I had a student who I thought was an excellent fit for the Burger King Corporation, so I called my friend Robert and set up an interview for him.

The day of the interview Robert calls me up and says to me "Dan, what is this a joke!"

"Bob what are you talking about" I say.

Robert then goes on to say, "Well today is April 1st, you know April Fool's Day" "It's not funny with the student you sent me" "It was embarrassing!"

I tell Robert, "I don't know what you mean. I did not play an April Fool's joke on you."

Then Robert goes on to tell me that the initial interview went well but when he got to the "Polygraph Test" he failed with flying colors.

Back then, most companies were giving prospective managers a polygraph test or a lie detector test as some may call it to determine someone's honesty and whether they may have committed a crime.

So, Robert then goes on to tell me that my student said that he had stolen money, shovels, and construction tools from his last job at Home Depot.

Moreover, Robert says" And did you know he is on Parole and cannot leave the state of New York?"

"Oh my God I exclaim! I don't believe it!"

Robert says, "I think all that teaching stuff has made you soft and gullible" "The next time you send me someone, if there is a next time, please check them out like you did when you were a manager – 'understand!"

I apologize to Robert and buy him dinner at the Cattleman Steak House. Hey sometimes you never know about people.

Polygraph Tests

Let me say a little more about Polygraph tests for those of you who may not know. A Polygraph test cannot test honesty, or whether someone committed a crime. Instead, it relies on the polygraph operator's questions before someone takes the test.

You see the operator will ask a series of questions. The Polygraph operator may ask for example:

"Did you ever steal from your employer?"

If you answer yes, the operator will ask you to explain your answer as what you stole and why, then when you take the Polygraph he will ask you the same questions he did in the interview.

The actual test begins by attaching devices that measure your blood pressure and heart rate. A spike in either of these when specific questions are asked may indicate that the person taking the polygraph may have lied. The questions asked during the test are the same questions you were asked at the interview and your answers while taking the test are either yes or no with no explanations.

So here is the thing. If you answered yes you stole from your employer during the actual polygraph you told the truth, so you did not lie. but you failed the test because you are a thief. Remember the interview that the operator conducted before the actual Polygraph test has the person's original answers.

The analysis of the Polygraph test is the operator's opinion based on the answers you gave during the interview and during the actual test as to spikes in your blood pressure or heart rate. It is based on the operator's opinion and not fact. As such it is unreliable and not admissible in a court room.

Also, most honest people are very nervous when it comes to taking a test that has you wired up to check for spikes in their heart rate and blood pressure and many people have higher than normal blood pressure readings when they go to their family doctor to check their blood pressure on a routine checkup. So many honest people fail the Polygraph test.

It is the savvy dishonest person that has no problem passing a lie detector test. I mean they are natural born liars.

Of course, the way to beat a Polygraph is to believe what you are saying is true even though it is not. If you really believe what you are saying is true then your body and the polygraph will also believe it to be true and you pass.

In my last year of college when I was completing my master's degree in business at the State University of New York (SUNY) I took a course called Business Ethics and one of the components of the course was to take an actual polygraph with the goal to see if you can beat the polygraph.

I give it a try. I take the test under the name of Errol Bullet and make up all his information, things like his date of birth, his address and so on.

I passed the test to the amazement of my professor and the class. Why did I pass? I passed the polygraph because I got my mind and body to believe what I said during the test was true –Simple!

Louisiana College

While I was at New York Restaurant School (NYRS) I received a phone call from a woman that I will call Sherry who is the program director of a Louisiana college that will remain nameless, and that she would like to fly to New York City and meet with me and discuss the possibility of developing a similar management program that we have at NYRS in her college in Louisiana.

I say okay I would be happy to meet with you. So, the next week she arrives in Manhattan and gets a room at the Hilton Hotel on west 54th street.

After work I go to the hotel and wait in the lobby for her. She sees me and walks up to me and introduces herself to me and I do the same. She is about forty years old, tall, possibly 6 feet, a redhead with a slender shape and a genuine southern accent.

"I am just starving, let's go to dinner and we can talk about the management program over dinner my treat." She says to me.

"Okay" Do you like Italian food?" I ask

"Eye-Talian" I just love everything Eye-Talian" she says.

So, we get in a cab, and go to Café Fiorello located at 1900 Broadway, just off Lincoln Center. Café Fiorello is a sophisticated, wood-paneled restaurant with outdoor seating located in the front of the restaurant and known for its thin-crust pizzas and classic Italian main courses.

She orders the chicken parmigiana, and I order spaghetti pomodoro and we get a bottle of Montepulciano d'Abruzzo.

As we eat, I tell her how successful the NYRS management program has been and that we have agreements with restaurants to pre-hire students before they graduate.

"What about the curriculum?" Do you have a curriculum you can give me?" she asks

I tell her I can write a new curriculum specific to Louisiana college's needs if you want and it will take me about a month to complete.

By now we are on our second bottle of Montepulciano d'Abruzzo and she says, "I need a restaurant curriculum now I'm afraid."

"I can give you $25,000.00 for the NYRS curriculum and anything else you may want." She says with a smile.

"I'm not really looking to hire you to develop a curriculum, I want the New York restaurant School's curriculum." "I mean Dan, you could just make a copy of the entire NYRS curriculum at Staples and it's an easy $25,0000 in your pocket she says as she sips her wine.

I look at her and say, "I don't know, I mean it's the NYRS curriculum really, it's not mine."

I tell her I really need to think about this, I mean it's not too ethical.

She pours the last of the wine into our glasses and says "Well, you know Dan, the education business is a dog-eat-dog business" Sherry says in her southern drawl.

"Why should I hire someone to write the curriculum and then I still must test it out when I could just get a copy from you." See what I mean Dan" Sherry says to me as she sips her wine.

"Listen, why don't we go back to my hotel; we can have a few drinks and I'll write you a check made out to cash for $35,000.00". She says as she rubs her leg with mine. "It my final offer Dan, what do you say?"

"It's really a tempting offer Sherry, I don't know, I need to think about it, I mean it's not mine to give."

I tell her as I swallow the last drop of wine from my glass.

"Well, I check out of the Hilton hotel at 11:00 am. If you decide to give up the curriculum just give me a call and I'll be waiting with a check for $35,000.00 and a bottle of champagne to seal the deal.

 Otherwise, I'm back in Louisiana on the next plane out of LaGuardia airport." I am in room 1404.

I hail a cab for her, and she heads back to the hotel. I decided to walk home since I have an apartment on 62nd street only a few blocks from the restaurant.

I'm pondering that it's not ethnical and besides if it gets out that I sold the curriculum I could be fired.

I have been working at the NYRS now for almost fifteen years and I really liked working here. I loved teaching and I felt a real sense of purpose. So, when I get home I call sherry and decline her offer.

The Art Institute of New York City

In 2001, the New York Restaurant School was sold to Art Institutes, which was part of the Education Management Corporation. At that time, Education Management was the largest for-profit college group with over 50 colleges in the in United States.

The Art Institute under Education Management expanded its college course offerings to include Fashion, design, and media courses and soon started paying less attention to their meat and potatoes program, Culinary Arts and Restaurant management and more attention to their non-culinary programs.

As a group, our instructors decided to form a union and become part of the United Federated of Teachers (UFT).

Education management did everything they legally could to prevent us from forming a union, however we were steadfast and became unionized.

THE ART INSTITUTE OF NEW YORK CITY CHAPTER

UNITED FEDERATION OF TEACHERS
Local 2, American Federation of Teachers, AFL-CIO
260 Park Avenue South, New York, NY 10010, (212) 777-7500

UFT Officers

Randi Weingarten, President
Ronald C. Jones, Secretary
Mel Aaronson, Treasurer
Elizabeth Langiulli, Assistant Secretary
Mona Romain, Assistant Treasurer

Vice Presidents
Carmen Alvarez
Michelle Bodden
Frank Carucci
Richard Farkas
David Sherman
Frank Volpicella

AiNYC/UFT Chapter Negotiating Committee

Steve Levitt
Chapter Leader

Gerald J. Gliber
Delegate

Toni L. D'Onofrio
Daniel F. Golio
John Gilmore
Stephen N. Hornstein

Lucille Swaim
UFT Coordinator of Negotiations

Art Institute UFT Contract

For those of you who may be interested in forming a union the first step would be to contact a union organizer, for us we contacted the United Federation of Teachers (UFT).

Next you need to have at least thirty percent of the workers sign a union authorization card which then allows you to file a petition with the National Labor Relations Board (NLRB) to hold a union election. You then need fifty percent of the workforce to vote yes plus one employee to form a union.

Okay you are now a union, and your employer must legally collectively bargain with the union and its union representatives.

Our school formed a collective bargaining committee, and I was asked to be on that committee to negotiate our union contract. During my time at Art Institute, I successfully negotiated three of the school's union contracts

Collective Bargaining

Collective bargaining is the process in which working people, through their unions, negotiate contracts with their employers to determine their terms of employment, including pay, benefits, hours, leave, job health and safety policies, ways to balance work and family, and more.

NYRS Chapter of UFT

In collective bargaining, a "last, best and final offer" is a formal proposal that one side presents to the other and includes all benefits and compromises. This is usually done to allow union members to vote to accept or reject an employer's best-case proposal.

As union members our teaching load was reduced and I had free time on my hands so during my free time I picked up some part-time work.

The Peoples Republic Of China

One day I got a call from a graduate of the college who was opening a series of fast-food Chinese restaurants, sort of like Panda Express which is an American fast food restaurant chain that specializes in American Chinese cuisine.

In any event he had a friend named George that was putting together an educational tour for the provincial Governors and the Ministry of Labour of The Peoples Republic of China and said that he gave my name and telephone to his friend because I would be a good fit for this sort of thing. After a brief conversation with his friend George, an Asian businessman with connections to the Chinese government, I was appointed.

I was hired to give lectures on the development and implementation of business organizations within the Provinces and well as the role of unions and labor management relations in business.

China was undergoing a period of expansion and business entrepreneurship. China was much different than the United States in terms of labor unions and while they had labor unions they were controlled by the state.

Ministry of Labour

In any event for a period of two years I would meet with either the governors of the provinces or the Ministry of Labour of China to discuss and lecture on these business topics.

Lectures were usually held at the 'Sheraton Hotel in Flushing Queens, New York and I remember one day as I was waiting for the congregation of the Ministry of Labour to arrive I was in the lobby of the hotel making a phone call.

And low and behold who walks into the lobby is Gary, one of my former students. I overheard his conversation, and it is obvious that he is applying for some type of assistant manager position at the hotel.

As he comes closer he stops dead in his tracks, sees me and I hear him say "Yes I worked for Dan Golio, and as a matter of fact – there he is right over there!"

We shook hands and Gary introduced me to the management of the hotel, I then went on to offer support for Gary telling them that Gary was an excellent assistant manager, and I would be glad to write a letter of recommendation for him.

With that the congregation arrives and I leave with the Ministry of Labour.

Lecturing to the Ministry of China was a unique experience because I did not speak Chinese, so an interpreter was provided. I had to speak in slow sentences and stop every two sentences for the interpreter to get my lectures accurately interpreted.

劳 动 部 教 育 培 训 中 心

Daniel F. Golio
New York Restaurant School

Dear Sir.   Dec. 22th, 1995

I hereby wish to express on behalf the Educational Training Center of the Ministry of Labour, our sincere thanks to you and your
school for the friendly sentiments and kind
arrangements during our Center's delegations
in U.S.A. Meanwhile, I am very pleased to
invite you and some your colleagues to visit
China at your convenience in 1996 in order to
have lecture and study exchange and to
promote the cooperation relations between the
two institutions.

Looking forward to your reply.

Sincerely yours,

Sun Lianjie
Director
Educational Training Center

Letter Ministry of Labour

After the lecture the governors asked excellent
questions and it was an enjoyable experience for all.

I remember this one time we were in a lecture room and the ceiling started to leak badly so I called the banquet department of the hotel, which is the department that usually rents lecture rooms, and asked them to send someone to fix the leak or move us to another room.

Soon the lecture doors open and Gary walks in and he tells me that the hotel hired him minutes after we met that time in the lobby. He switched us to another lecture room and then invited me to dine with him and his wife in their Brooklyn brownstone which I did.

With free time on our hands Harry and I decided to do some consulting while we were teaching at Art Institutes of NYC, so we formed a consulting company called Restaurant Consultants LLC, with a specialty in loss prevention.

As loss prevention consultants we went undercover for such concerns as the world famous Tatou Night Club in New York City. Oscars Steak House, Playwright Irish Pubs, the McDonald's, and Burger King corporations.

Basically, we looked for design flaws and control system errors that would give employees the opportunity to steal.

While places like the Playwright Irish Pubs, and the fast-food establishments had either bartenders, waitresses or cashiers not ringing up sales, the Tatou nightclub was unique to say the least.

Tatou Night Club

Tatou was located at 151 East 50th Street, Manhattan. The inside of the club resembled a mini-opera house. The upscale restaurant, live music and loud conversation made it one of the top dance clubs of the 1990's.

The location had a lot of history behind it, before it became the Club Tatou it was the old Versailles Club, where Desi Arnaz once led the band, and soon won its own reputation as an elegant restaurant, nightspot, and celebrity hangout. It is at Tatou that President Bill Clinton played the saxophone and Mariah Carey had her first professional showcase.

Our company was hired to find out why revenue was down, so Harry and I went undercover, eating in the restaurant, going to the club, dancing, and drinking at the bar. I know you are saying to yourself, wow this is a hard job, all that partying must have been very hard on you guys. Well, it's all as part of our investigation and besides somebody must do it.

Club Tatou

The only thing that stood out was the door cover, which at the time was twenty dollars. At the door, people collecting the cover were stealing in plain sight. They would pocket every other cover, you know, twenty dollars for the club and twenty dollars for the people collecting the cover at the door.

Harry and I estimated that on any given Thursday or Friday night there were between 500 to 1,000 people in and out of the club.

At a cover of twenty dollars per person that adds up to $10,000 to $20,000 per night and not the $5,000 the club received at the door. It was obvious that $10,000 to $15,000 was being stolen.

But that was not the kicker. When Harry and I sat through hundreds of hours of surveillance tape what we found was astounding.

As we sat and watched one evening we saw something strange. About an hour after club Tatou closed, the doors opened again, and people started coming into Tatou. However, Tatou was officially closed.

Dishonest employees had reopened the club as an after-hours joint, with a full bar and food. They charged the same cover of twenty dollars at the door and for that price, people would eat and drink all night at the company's expense.

This went on literally all night every Thursday, Friday and Saturday night, the busy times in most restaurants and clubs. At the end of the night the employees split up the take between them, cleaned up club Tatou and left.

Our surveillance continued for one month to establish the pattern of behavior of the dishonest employees.

When we presented our finding to management they were in disbelief.

Harry said to management "Don't you guys look at the surveillance tapes to see what's going on in your establishment?"

"Not really" was the management's response.

I said to management "You guys are getting ripped off, you are losing thousands of dollars at the door and your nighttime employees are doing whatever they want. It's a free for all here in Tatou"

Harry said, "You need controls, inventory, cash and beverage." Do you want us to set it up for you?"

The management said no, they will handled it and paid us the rest of our consulting fee.

I told the management of Tatou "Listen if you don't implement the procedures we advised you will be out of business in six months or less"

"Yea, don't worry we got this" they said

Anyway, it appeared that club tatou did not take our advice because the club closed almost to the day that I predicted. I mean what's the point in hiring professionals to help correct problems if you don't take their advice. – go figure!

Harry and I were also hired to write the first formal culinary and management curriculum for New York State Certification for The Institute of Culinary Education. Later they would go on to rewrite that curriculum to better suit the needs of the school and its students. However, it was the curriculum that Harry and I wrote that granted the school state approval.

By now I have been teaching mostly business management classes and courses in wine appreciation.

Dan Golio School Publicity Post card

I hold certificates from both the French and German wine councils and have published a book on wine entitled "The Fundamentals of Wine", so the Art Institute of New York City thought it would be a good idea to publicize it.

As time went I was the most senior instructor at the Art Institute of New York City with almost twenty-five years of teaching experience at the school.

In our department we had top notch instructors in

both Culinary and Restaurant Management. Our school was rated among the top ten Culinary and Restaurant schools on the East coast. Second only to the Culinary Institute of America and maybe New York Technical College.

The Party's Over

However, trouble was brewing over the horizon. As mentioned earlier, Education Management had diversified its courses to include fashion, design, and media all of which was a major failure. Education Management spent hundreds of thousands of dollars in developing and promoting courses that had little chance of success.

Simply because New York City is home to two major Fashion Schools: Fashion Institute of technology and Parsons School of Design at the New School for Social Research. Both are premier in their class and well branded - DUH

For media and film production, the top school in New York City is the New York Film Academy with the New School for Social Research's media College second.

Culinary courses were put on the back burner at this time and restaurant management classes were starting to dwindle.

The meat and potatoes of the Art Institute of NYC has always been the Culinary and Restaurant management classes without which the school will fail.

I have always had a sixth sense about people and business so in my gut I knew the school would close.

At our annual instructor meeting in 2009 I confronted management about their plan to close the culinary and restaurant management program and focus on its other less lucrative programs. Their response was less than reassuring and getting a "bullshit" answer as to whether our Culinary and Restaurant Management programs were on the chopping block I told the UFT of my beliefs. The UFT thought I was overreacting, but I had to follow my instinct.

While Art Institute instructors were diligent and sincere in their dealings with students and had a strong desire to see their students succeed in any endeavor they may undertake, the admissions department and Education Management did not share the same views.

In fact, the Art Institutes had created a boiler room style recruitment and sales format; whereby the goal of the school was to enroll students at any cost.

So, in 2010 with approximately twenty-five years of teaching experience with the NYRS and then Art institutes I resigned.

It seems my gut instincts were correct because shortly after in 2011, the Art Institute of NYC and its other fifty institutions were involved in a United States Department of Justice investigation and lawsuit alleging both illegal recruitment practices and fraudulent receipt of $11 billion in federal and state financial aid money.

All in all, over forty schools were closed because of the DOJ investigation, and looking back my sixth sense about people and business helped me in avoiding this unfortunate scandal.

In 2022, the Art Institute was one of 153 institutions included in student loan cancellation due to alleged fraud. The class action was brought by a group of more than 200,000 student borrowers, assisted by the Project on Predatory Student Lending, part of the Legal Services Center of Harvard Law School.

Conclusion

During my career in the Restaurant and Hospitality business I believe that I have done and accomplished more than most people in the hospitality industry.

According to a recent survey 35% of restaurant managers quit in their first year on the job and only last approximately two years before they change fields completely.

Chefs are no different, with salaries ranging from $50,000.00 to $75,000.00 per year, the turnover rate is high. There are exceptions of course, Emeril Lagasse or Wolfgang Puck to name a few who makes the big bucks, but they are few and far between. Statically only 10 percent of the chefs working today make over $100,000.00 a year.

My progression in the restaurant and hospitality industry has allowed me to see it all: From working as a dishwasher to prep and line cook to advancing to the position of Sous Chef, I have seen it all in the Back Of the House. (B.O.H.) as well as the Front Of The House (F.O.H). From Assistant manager to Director of Food and Beverage to owning a catering and consulting company and finally to instructor, the hospitality industry is in my blood.

As I mentioned before it is a very high stress industry, you are basically married to your job. Most general managers feel that they do not get enough quality time with family and friends.

When you are younger, hanging out with your co-workers until the early morning hours may be enjoyable and exciting, but as you get older and lucky enough to get married, you want to spend quality time with family and friends.

So, for me teaching in the hospitality industry was the natural progression and I had made some excellent investments and was in excellent shape financially when I decided to retire from actively working in the hospitality field.

So, when I retired I traveled first by cruising then by plane taking trips to Europe especially Italy and Rome. I mean I try to go to 'Rome at least once a year but the Eternal City has been invaded by tourists who believe that spaghetti sauce out of a jar is real "Eye-Talian"

It is liked to a scene from the movie "Goodfellows", where Actor Ray Liotta is in the witness protection program living somewhere in the Mid-West and orders spaghetti with marinara sauce and gets egg noodles with ketchup instead.

So rather than sit in my rocking chair and rock back and forth I decided to write about the hospitality industry, food, wine, and management because the hospitality industry is still in my blood.

About The Author

Daniel Golio was born in East Harlem, on Pleasant Avenue in New York City. An author, teacher, and restaurant consultant. Mr. Golio started his culinary career as a Sous Chef in Italian restaurants in New York City and then went on to serve as the Director of Food and Beverage for such concerns as the Biltmore, and Roosevelt hotels in New York City; as well as the Food and Beverage Director for JFK International airport.

As owner of Manhattan Parties, an upscale event and catering company, Dan has planned events for the television show Entertainment Tonight, and such companies as the Ford Modeling Agency, Cover Girl Makeup, Petrossian Caviar NYC, the Bank of Italy, WBLS Radio in New York and countless television commercials and music videos.

Mr. Golio holds certificates in wine appreciation from both the French and German Councils and for over twenty-five years has taught wine appreciation classes for the New School of Social Research and the Art Institute of NYC. He holds a degree in Culinary Arts from New York technical College, a bachelor's degree in economics and a master's degree in business from the State University of New York

Although semi-retired, Dan has taken to writing books about food and wine and crime novels set in New York City.

Other Books by Daniel Golio

The Fundamentals of Wine
From My Mother's Kitchen
Pleasant Avenue: The way it Was

Available at Amazon.com, Barnes and Noble and fine books stores worldwide